D0138744

Integrating Women's Studies into the Curriculum

Integrating Women's Studies into the Curriculum

An Annotated Bibliography

Compiled by
Susan Douglas Franzosa
and Karen A. Mazza

Bibliographies and Indexes in Education, Number 1

Greenwood Press
Westport, Connecticut • London, England

Library of Congress Cataloging in Publication Data

Franzosa, Susan Douglas.
  Integrating women's studies into the curriculum.

  (Bibliographies and indexes in education, ISSN 0742-
6917 ; no. 1)
  Includes index.
  1. Women's studies—United States—Bibliography.
2. Interdisciplinary approach in education—United States
—Bibliography. 3. Universities and colleges—United
States—Curricula—Planning—Bibliography. I. Mazza,
Karen A. II. Title. III. Series.
  Z7964.U49F73 1984   016.3054'07'11   84-12815
  [HQ1181.U5]
  ISBN 0-313-24482-0 (lib. bdg.)

Library of Congress Catalog Card Number: 84-12815
ISBN: 0-313-24482-0
ISSN: 0742-6917

First published in 1984

Greenwood Press
A division of Congressional Information Service, Inc.
88 Post Road West, Westport, Connecticut 06881

Printed in the United States of America

10 9 8 7 6 5 4 3 2 1

CONTENTS

PREFACE

The growth of an extensive body of scholarship on women in the past ten to fifteen years has heightened awareness of the need to revise existing knowledge in the traditional disciplines so that a more balanced, accurate, and equitable curriculum might be developed. The impact of this scholarship has encouraged the growth of numerous equity projects across the country that seek to transform existing curriculum and develop new courses that are informed by feminist research. This bibliography is designed to serve as a resource guide for universities and secondary schools involved in these curriculum transformation efforts.

What distinguishes <u>Integrating Women's Studies into the Curriculum</u> from other bibliographies in the new scholarship on women is its organizational theme and rationale. A transformation of the curriculum requires that scholars and teachers identify inequities within their field as well as work toward the development of new perspectives on disciplinary content, research methods, and teaching. The over 500 sources included here were selected with this in mind. They specifically address the issues of bias and exclusion within the traditional disciplines, evaluate or apply emerging feminist research methods and theoretical perspectives, and present strategies designed to integrate women and their contributions and experiences within the curriculum.

A few comments about the organizational format of the bibliography are in order. The first two chapters contain entries that provide resources and general background information on integrating Women's Studies into the general curriculum. Administrators will find these two chapters particularly helpful and may wish to refer to Chapter II for sources that provide information on the nature and purposes of Women's Studies and the organizational changes that support and enhance curriculum integration efforts.

The seven chapters that follow correspond to traditional disciplinary clusters. This organizational pattern, however, is not meant to solidify already entrenched disciplinary divisions. Instead, we hope readers will come to understand and appreciate the creative and vital interdisciplinary nature of much feminist scholarship. The advantage of a disciplinary organizational pattern, on the other hand, is that it allows readers to begin work in an area in which they are already knowledgeable. Each disciplinary cluster is further subdivided into the following subsections of annotated entries: "Women in the Profession" (their entrance and status in the field); "Reconceptualizing the Discipline" (how the discipline could be changed); "Special Issues" (topics relevant to women's scholarship in the particular discipline); and "Curriculum Strategies." Citations within each section focus on the years from 1976 to 1983, although earlier works of a classic or unique nature also have been included. Sources for works that do not appear in <u>Books in Print</u> are listed in the "Directory of Sources" at the end of the volume.

The initial research for this study was funded by the General Education Committee of the University of New Hampshire and sponsored by the Women's Studies Program at the same institution. Beyond the needs of our own institution, it is hoped that all interested educators will be able to draw on the resources presented here. For some, the references in the bibliography will be a valuable introduction to Women's Studies and how it relates to one's own research area. For others, who may already be familiar with research on women within their own field, it will suggest further possibilities for interdisciplinary teaching and scholarship in Women's Studies.

S.D.F.
K.A.M.

ACKNOWLEDGMENTS

We are indebted to many people for their contributions to the project. A grant from the University of New Hampshire's General Education Committee supported our initial research. Funds from the University of Maine at Orono's WEEA project made it possible to attend conferences at Orono ("Moving Toward a Balanced Curriculum III, May 17-18, 1983) and at Wheaton College ("Toward a Balanced Curriculum," June 22-24, 1983) at which we were able to consult with other scholars involved in curriculum integration efforts. Special thanks are due to Cathryn Adamsky of the Women's Studies Program at the University of New Hampshire, who encouraged us to extend the project, and to Jane Roland Martin, Carol Goodenow, and Joan Mundy for their thoughtful suggestions on sources. We are grateful too, to Alfreda Furnas and Bess Franzosa for their assistance in locating materials and indexing. Finally, with appreciation and respect for a job well done, we wish to acknowledge and thank Kit Nardello, who typed the manuscript, for her invaluable assistance.

INTRODUCTION

A search of relevant indexes quickly reveals the abundance of knowledge that has been produced on women. The task in constructing a bibliography of this nature is to frame a rationale for the selection of bibliographic entries. The perspective taken here is derived from the sociology of curriculum and from recent works in feminist curriculum theory that urge educators to question the assumptions used to guide the process of constructing and distributing knowledge.1 This perspective helps educators understand both the obvious and the often invisible influences of sexism, classism, and racism on the traditional curriculum and enlightens strategies for correcting curricular exclusion and existing imbalances. Our intent in using this perspective is to select entries that will provide readers with information that will familiarize them with major assumptions, theories, research methodologies, and teaching practices within their own fields that have been critiqued by the new scholarship on women. This information will enable interested and concerned faculty to analyze their disciplines, integrate Women's Studies into the curriculum, and reconceptualize the knowledge and theories they disseminate through research and teaching.

Reconceptualizing Knowledge

A reconceptualization of knowledge is central to a gender balanced transformation of the curriculum. Reconceptualization necessitates the critical practice of questioning the assumptions, categories, and paradigms that have dominated the definition and production of knowledge in the past as well as those that will influence what will come to be valued as knowledge in the future. Equity issues can be considered at five major points in the production of knowledge. These points are knowledge selection, knowledge construction, knowledge distribution, knowledge transmission, and knowledge legitimation.2

Knowledge selection is the easiest and most obvious point at which bias and exclusion in the production of knowledge and in the construction of curriculums can be recognized. In this phase of the process, feminist scholars investigate why particular knowledge has been selected and other knowledge omitted. They examine whose knowledge is being represented and what interests or values are being served by this selection. The fundamental question asked is: Does this specific course of study include and accurately portray the experience of women and minorities?

Equity issues become apparent in the process of knowledge construction when feminist scholars examine established assumptions about acceptable research methodology, modes of theorizing, and references, and question whether or not they are helpful for the construction of knowledge relevant to women's experience. Research designs that exclude women as subjects or that reject the legitimacy of qualitative forms of research have long been barriers that excluded women's reports about their own experience of the world. At this point in the reconceptualization process, educators must ask themselves: Do the existing research procedures, tools, and references allow us to accurately research and report women's experience in our fields? What are the methodological barriers within the discipline that limit the construction of knowledge about women's experience?

A second and crucial element of knowledge construction to which faculty concerned with curricular equity need to give special consideration is interpretation and organization of research findings into theories and conceptual frameworks. All too often knowledge has been presented as though it was objective and final, without recognition that knowledge is subject to differing interpretations that have important social and political consequences. As contemporary philosophers of science have shown, this problem exists in all fields, including technology and science.[3]

More specifically, with respect to knowledge about women, disciplinary theories have often distorted knowledge about women because they have interpreted women's experience according to explanations that are more representative of male experience. Additionally, the categories that researchers typically explore have often ignored women's social situation, focusing instead on topics that are common to men's experience. When informed by modern feminist critique, the traditional structures and explanations of a discipline yield to theories that recover knowledge about women's experience and interpret it within new frameworks. The use of feminist perspectives leads to interpreting men's and women's experience, and reality itself, differently. However, it is in this area of interpretation that bias and exclusion in the conceptual and theoretical foundations of a discipline are often difficult to recognize, and readers are encouraged to explore this point with more specific reference to their own field by reading entries listed under sections marked by the subheading, "Reconceptualizing the Disciplines."

In the third area, knowledge distribution, feminist scholars explore the cultural, ideological, historical, and institutional factors that have influenced the distribution of knowledge in a discipline with respect to sex, race, and social class. They ask who has historically had access to knowledge within the field and, what are the explicit and tacit contemporary barriers that continue to exclude or limit the interest or achievement of women. The underrepresentation of women in the maths and sciences and in areas of the public domain such as business, administration, and governance continues to be a special concern with regard to these issues. Awareness of these barriers calls for solutions that go beyond curriculum revision and involve institutional change. For example, in responding to this issue faculty may need to seek institutional support for changes in class size, teaching methods, advisement, and the development of special programs to meet specific needs.

The transmission of knowledge is also an area that involves issues that go beyond curriculum revision. Feminist scholars have realized that an equitable curriculum cannot be developed without also inquiring about how teaching methodology affects the education of women and minorities. To facilitate the search for equity, feminist scholars recommend that knowledge presented be considered from different points of view and that students should be encouraged to develop critical thinking skills. For example, pedagogical techniques and classroom social relationships recurrently recommended in feminist scholarship include: (1) encouraging students to critique the knowledge presented to them; (2) presenting knowledge in a way that facilitates students' ability to relate it to their personal experience and existing knowledge; (3) fostering the development of self-knowledge; (4) developing collaborative classroom social relationships that promote a spirit of inquiry; and (5) alerting students to how the social context in which they live influences the curriculum they are engaged in studying. Awareness of these pedagogical issues will enable faculty to rethink their approach to teaching in conjunction with course revision.

The fifth and final point in the knowledge production process, knowledge legitimation, refers to the evaluation of what is valid and acceptable in research. This factor operates correlatively with the other points. Here, feminist scholars encourage faculty to ask why some forms of language and inquiry are most highly regarded and dominate a field. They point out that researchers need to examine the processes by which professional associations, editorial boards, funding sources, and universities legitimize some forms of research and exclude others. For example, in many such arenas Women's Studies has not been considered legitimate research, and like women in general, it has been devalued without adequate examination of the bias implicit in the methods and policies that determine official sanction.

This brief introduction to major themes for consideration in reconceptualizing knowledge and transforming the curriculum is provided as a preview to the types of analysis used and issues raised in the entries selected for inclusion in this bibliography. In reading examples of the new scholarship on women, readers will not find quick solutions or easy formulas for curriculum revision. But, hopefully, they will find the challenge, excitement, and sense of purpose that comes from engaging in highly significant research that is itself a major aspect of a wider social transformation, one guided by the interests of truthfulness, justice, and equality.

NOTES

1. Michael W. Apple, <u>Education and Power</u> (Boston: Routledge and Kegan Paul 1982) and <u>Ideology and Curriculum</u> (Boston: Routledge and Kegan Paul, 1979); John Eggleston, <u>The Sociology of the School Curriculum</u> (Boston: Routledge and Kegan Paul, 1977); Henry Giroux, <u>Ideology, Culture and the Process of Schooling</u> (Philadelphia: Temple University Press,

1981); Madeleine R. Grumet, "Conception, Contradiction and Curriculum," <u>Journal of Curriculum Theorizing</u> 3, 1 (1981): 287-98; Barry A. Kaufman and Gail M. Kaufman, "Reconstructing Child Development for Curriculum Studies: Critical and Feminist Perspectives," <u>Journal of Curriculum Theorizing</u> 2, 2 (1980): 245-68; Janet L. Miller, "The Sound of Silence Breaking: Feminist Pedagogy and Curriculum Theory," <u>Journal of Curriculum Theorizing</u> 4, 1 (1982): 5-11 and "Women: The Evolving Educational Consciousness," <u>Journal of Curriculum Theorizing</u> 2, 1 (1980): 223-47; James B. Macdonald and Susan Colberg Macdonald, "Gender, Values, and Curriculum," <u>Journal of Curriculum Theorizing</u> 3, 1 (1981): 299-304; Barbara S. Mitrano, "Feminism and Curriculum Theory: Implications for Teacher Education," <u>Journal of Curriculum Theorizing</u> 3, 2 (1981): 5-85; Rachel Sharp, <u>Knowledge Ideology and the Politics of Schooling: Towards a Marxist Analysis of Education</u> (Boston: Routledge and Kegan Paul, 1980); Peter Maas Taubman, "Gender and Curriculum: Discourse and the Politics of Sexuality," <u>Journal of Curriculum Theorizing</u> 4, 1 (1982): 12-87; and Sandra Wallenstein, "Notes Toward a Feminist Curriculum Theory," <u>Journal of Curriculum Theorizing</u> 1, 1 (1979): 186-90.

2. The British sociologist of education Basil Bernstein was among the first to suggest these theoretical foci and has done extensive work in the area that can be found in his <u>Class, Codes and Control, Vol. 3: Towards a Theory of Educational Transmissions</u> (London: Routledge and Kegan Paul, 1975). See also: Michael F. D. Young, <u>Knowledge and Control: New Directions for the Sociology of Education</u> (London: Collier-Macmillan, 1977).

3. Thomas Kuhn, <u>The Structure of Scientific Revolutions</u> (Chicago: University of Chicago Press, 1970).

Integrating Women's Studies into the Curriculum

I.
BIBLIOGRAPHIC STUDIES
AND RESOURCE GUIDES

Beginning in the late 1960s there was a dramatic increase in the publication of bibliographic studies and resource guides dealing with women's issues, contributions, roles and status. This increase corresponded to the growth of the women's movement on college and university campuses and reflected a growing awareness that women and their works had been neglected within the traditional curriculum. The first reference guides that began to appear were the result of attempts to recover the contributions of women in particular fields of study. Useful bibliographies of "women in" a special discipline or "women of" a specific era or geographical region were compiled. Canonical lists of "great men" and "forefathers" were challenged and revised.

As the interest in a new scholarship on women grew, bibliographic studies asked new research questions and began to suggest alternative ways of organizing knowledge. Reference works structured according to interdisciplinary thematic issues relevant to women became more frequent. Students and scholars were thus given easier initial access to scholarly resources on women and the family, women and work, culture, politics, religion, sex roles, equity and education. Several scholarly journals began to focus attention on research on women within their disciplines. Notably, the journal SIGNS fostered and sustained dissemination efforts by regularly publishing critical bibliographic appraisals of the literature, or "Essay Reviews," by leading scholars in each field of study.

Current work in Women's Studies resources has produced several useful guides and bibliographies designed to aid teachers and students in the reconceptualization of the traditional academic curriculum. These continuing efforts indicate a desire to recover the old as well as to foster the new; to create and share revised frameworks for research and teaching.

The bibliographies and resource guides listed here are of several types. Citations include: (1) works that compile references to forgotten or excluded female contributors in Art, Music, Film, Science, Medicine, Mathematics, Literature, the Social Sciences, Philosophy and History; (2) surveys of women's status and role during particular historical periods and in specific cultural contexts; (3) thematic studies of women in society, economics, religion, politics and education, and within particular

vocations; (4) works dealing with the women's movement and Women's
Studies; and (5) reference guides to curricular materials and resources.

1. Astin, Helen S., et al. SEX ROLES: A RESEARCH BIBLIOGRAPHY.
   Rockville, MD: National Institute of Mental Health, 1975.

   > Extensive guide to the literature prior to 1975 compiled as
   > part of a project for the National Institute of Mental Health.
   > 362 pages.

2. Bachmann, Donna G. and Sherry Piland. WOMEN ARTISTS: AN HIS-
   TORICAL, CONTEMPORARY, AND FEMINIST BIBLIOGRAPHY. Metuchen, NJ:
   Scarecrow Press, 1978.

   > Includes annotated citations to general works and biographies
   > of 160 women artists from the fifteenth-century to 1930. 323
   > pages.

3. Ballou, Patricia K. WOMEN: A BIBLIOGRAPHY OF BIBLIOGRAPHIES.
   Boston, MA: G. K. Hall, 1980.

   > Lists and selectively annotates 500 bibliographies published
   > between 1970 and 1979. Includes women's movement publications
   > as well as scholarly books and articles. 155 pages.

4. Block, Adrienne Fried and Carol Neuls-Bates. WOMEN IN AMERICAN
   MUSIC: A BIBLIOGRAPHY OF MUSIC AND LITERATURE. Westport, CT:
   Greenwood Press, 1979.

   > Includes citations to women and music, biographies of women
   > musicians and references to their works in literature and
   > poetry. 302 pages.

5. Borenstein, Audrey. OLDER WOMEN IN 20-CENTURY AMERICA: A SELECTED
   ANNOTATED BIBLIOGRAPHY. New York, NY: Garland Publishing, 1982.

   > Deals with women over 40 in 20th-century North America. Topics
   > covered are interdisciplinary. Includes books, essays, and
   > journal articles. 351 pages.

6. Buhle, Mari Jo. WOMEN AND THE AMERICAN LEFT: A GUIDE TO SOURCES.
   BOSTON, MA: G. K. Hall, 1983.

   > Annotated bibliography of sources dealing with the relationship
   > of class and gender in theories and strategies of social change.
   > Contains general works and histories, autobiographies and bio-
   > graphies, books and pamphlets, periodicals and works of fiction
   > arranged by time periods from 1871 to 1981. 281 pages.

7. Cantor, Aviva. BIBLIOGRAPHY ON THE JEWISH WOMAN: A COMPREHENSIVE
    AND ANNOTATED LISTING OF WORKS PUBLISHED 1900-1978. Fresh Meadows,
    NY: Biblio Press, 1982.

    Lists over six hundred citations of articles, books and mono-
    graphs. 97 pages.

8. Cardinale, Susan. ANTHOLOGIES BY AND ABOUT WOMEN: AN ANALYTICAL
    INDEX. Westport, CT: Greenwood Press, 1982.

    References to 300 anthologies on women's issues and collec-
    tions of women's writings. Includes author and content list-
    ing for each volume and subject and genre indexes. 282 pages.

9. Chinn, Phyllis Zweig. WOMEN IN SCIENCE AND MATH. Washington, DC:
    Office of Opportunities in Science, 1978.

    Bibliography with 400 citations of articles, books, journals,
    and bibliographies.

10. Cohen, Aaron I. INTERNATIONAL ENCYCLOPEDIA OF WOMEN COMPOSERS. New
    York, NY: Bowker, 1980.

    Includes 3700 biographies of women composers from ancient to
    modern times, titles of their works, appendix of sources and
    list of 1300 composers about whom little is known. 597 pages.

11. Coven, Brends. AMERICAN WOMEN DRAMATISTS OF THE TWENTIETH
    CENTURY: A BIBLIOGRAPHY. Metuchen, NJ: Scarecrow Press, 1982.

    Presents a brief general bibliography on women playwrights,
    followed by an alphabetically arranged list of individual
    author bibliographies. 237 pages.

12. Duke, Maurice, Jackson R. Bryer, and M. Thomas Inge. AMERICAN
    WOMEN WRITERS: BIBLIOGRAPHIC ESSAYS. Westport, CT: Greenwood
    Press, 1983.

    Collection of fourteen bibliographic essays on twenty-five
    American women writers ranging from Ann Bradstreet to con-
    temporary authors and poets. 434 pages.

13. Farr, Sidney Saylor. APPALACHIAN WOMEN: AN ANNOTATED BIBLIOGRAPHY.
    Lexington, KY: University Press of Kentucky, 1981.

    Compilation of 1300 monographs, chapters, articles and dis-
    sertations arranged by topical issues. Includes source list
    for oral history tapes. 187 pages.

14. Faunce, Patricia Spencer. WOMEN AND AMBITION: A BIBLIOGRAPHY.
    Metuchen, NJ: Scarecrow Press, 1980.

    Unannotated but extensive bibliography of over 10,000 cita-
    tions to books, articles and monographs on women and achieve-
    ment published between 1960 and 1976. Includes sections deal-
    ing with each academic discipline and profession. 695 pages.

15. Feinberg, Renee. WOMEN, EDUCATION, AND EMPLOYMENT: A BIBLI-
    OGRAPHY OF PERIODICAL CITATIONS, PAMPHLETS, NEWSPAPERS, AND
    GOVERNMENT DOCUMENTS, 1970-1980. Hamden, CT: Shoestring Press,
    1982.

    Covers publications from 1970 to 1980. Includes over 2500
    unannotated citations arranged by topic in two major sections;
    employment and education. 274 pages.

16. Frey, Linda, et al. WOMEN IN WESTERN EUROPEAN HISTORY: A SELECT
    CHRONOLOGICAL, GEOGRAPHICAL, AND TOPICAL BIBLIOGRAPHY FROM
    ANTIQUITY TO THE FRENCH REVOLUTION. Westport, CT: Greenwood
    Press, 1982.

    Compiles 6894 citations to monographs, books and journal
    articles by and about women and women's issues. 760 pages.

17. Froschl, Merle and Jane Williamson. FEMINIST RESOURCES FOR SCHOOLS
    AND COLLEGES: A GUIDE TO CURRICULAR MATERIALS. Old Westbury, NY:
    Feminist Press, 1977.

    References to works on sex differences in education, non-sexist
    teaching materials and texts, and bibliographies for the
    liberal arts disciplines. 67 pages.

18. Grimes, Janet. NOVELS IN ENGLISH BY WOMEN, 1891-1920: A PRELIMI-
    NARY CHECKLIST. New York, NY: Garland Publishing, 1981.

    Cites over 5000 authors and 15000 novels published in the
    United States and England. Annotates three quarters of the
    entries. 805 pages.

19. Haber, Barbara. WOMEN IN AMERICA: A GUIDE TO BOOKS, 1963-1975;
    WITH AN APPENDIX ON BOOKS PUBLISHED 1976-1979. Boston, MA: G. K.
    Hall, 1981.

    Includes topically arranged selectively annotated citations to
    450 non-fiction items on women's issues. 202 pages.

20. Hinding, Andrea, ed. WOMEN'S HISTORY SOURCES: A GUIDE TO ARCHIVES
    AND MANUSCRIPT COLLECTIONS IN THE UNITED STATES. Vols. 1 and 2.
    New York, NY: Bowker, 1979.

    Volume I contains a listing of over 18000 collections arranged
    by state and includes brief descriptions of content and
    physical conditions. 1114 pages. Volume II is arranged by
    subject and author and cross referenced to items in Volume I.
    391 pages.

21. HISTORY OF WOMEN. Woodbridge, CT: Research Publications Incorpo-
    rated, 1977.

    Microfilm collection of approximately 8500 volumes of printed
    books and pamphlets, 200 pamphlet titles, 117 periodical
    titles, 80000 pages of manuscript items in 32 groups, 800
    photographs, with a bibliography index. 408 pages.

22. Ireland, Norma Olin. INDEX TO WOMEN OF THE WORLD FROM ANCIENT
    TO MODERN TIMES: BIOGRAPHIES AND PORTRAITS. Westwood, MA: F. W.
    Faxon Company, 1970. 573 pages.

23. Kennedy, Susan Estabrook. AMERICA'S WHITE WORKING-CLASS WOMEN: AN
    HISTORICAL BIBLIOGRAPHY. New York, NY: Garland Publishing, 1981.

    Contains books, articles, government documents, and disserta-
    tions to explore the relationship between race, class, and
    gender in the lives of white working-class women. Arranged by
    historical periods and subtopics. Annotated. 253 pages.

24. Knaster, Meri. WOMEN IN SPANISH AMERICA: AN ANNOTATED BIBLIOGRAPHY
    FROM PRE-CONQUEST TO CONTEMPORARY TIMES. Boston, MA: G. K. Hall,
    1977.

    Extensive bibliography of monographs, journal articles and
    books sectioned according to academic disciplines and
    historical themes. 695 pages.

25. Krichmar, Albert. THE WOMEN'S MOVEMENT IN THE SEVENTIES: AN
    INTERNATIONAL ENGLISH - LANGUAGE BIBLIOGRAPHY. Metuchen, NJ:
    Scarecrow Press, 1977.

    Annotated bibliography of general, cultural and literary,
    economic, educational, legal and political, psychological,
    religious and philosophical, scientific and technological,
    sociological and anthropoplogical studies organized by regions
    of the world. 875 pages.

26. Leavitt, Judith A. WOMEN IN MANAGEMENT, 1970-1979: AN ANNOTATED BIBLIOGRAPHY AND SOURCE LIST. Phoenix, AZ: Oryx Press, 1982.

    Citations to books, articles and media coverage of items that document the progress and obstacles of women in business and management. Includes 800 sources arranged in twenty topical categories. 216 pages.

27. Lerner, Gerda. BIBLIOGRAPHY IN THE HISTORY OF AMERICAN WOMEN. Bronxville, NY: Sarah Lawrence College Press, 1978.

    Compilation of contemporary and classic works by and about women in American history.

28. McFeeley, Mary Drake. WOMEN'S WORK IN BRITAIN AND AMERICA FROM THE 90's to WWI: AN ANNOTATED BIBLIOGRAPHY. Boston, MA: G. K. Hall, 1982.

    Selectively annotated introductory overview of sources, including citations for journal articles, essays and pamphlets published between 1880 and 1980. 140 pages.

29. McKee, Kathleen Burke. WOMEN'S STUDIES: A GUIDE TO REFERENCE SOURCES. Storrs, CT: University of Connecticut, 1977.

    Annotates 364 citations including the University of Connecticut's Alternative Press Collection plus books and pamphlets from women's movement publishers on Third World women, socialist feminism, lesbianism, and other feminist issues. 112 pages.

30. Nordquist, Joan. AUDIOVISUALS FOR WOMEN. Jefferson, NC: McFarland, 1980.

    Citations for films, slides and tapes on women's issues and history. 153 pages.

31. Oakes, Elizabeth and Kathleen Sheldon. GUIDE TO SOCIAL SCIENCE RESOURCES IN WOMEN'S STUDIES. Santa Barbara, CA: ABC-CLIO, 1978.

    Includes books, bibliographies, collections of articles in journals, and other resources to assist in research and in the organization of courses on women. Annotated. 162 pages.

32. Parker, Franklin and Betty Parker. WOMEN'S EDUCATION; A WORLD VIEW: AN ANNOTATED BIBLIOGRAPHY OF DOCTORAL DISSERTATIONS. Westport, CT: Greenwood Press, 1979.

Compiles international citations by academic discipline.   470
pages.

33. _____. WOMEN'S EDUCATION A WORLD VIEW: AN ANNOTATED BIBLIO-
GRAPHY OF BOOKS AND REPORTS. Westport, CT: Greenwood Press, 1981.

Includes references to over 4000 books, reports and monographs
on all areas of women's education and training. 689 pages.

34. Reinhartz, Shulamit, Marti Bombeck and Janet Wright. "Methodolog-
ical Issues In Feminist Research: A Bibliography of Literature in
Women's Studies, Sociology and Psychology." WOMEN'S STUDIES INTER-
NATIONAL FORUM, 6, 4 (1983), 437-454.

Topically arranged, selectively annotated and chronologically
listed references to British and American books and scholarly
articles published between 1951 and 1982. Includes introductory commentaries.

35. RESOURCES IN WOMEN'S EDUCATIONAL EQUITY. Women's Educational Equity
Network (Sponsored by the US Department of Education). San Francisco,
CA: Farwest Laboratory for Educational Research and Development, 1976 -

Extensive annual resource guides drawing on 12 data bases.
Complete subject and author indexes.

36. Sims-Wood, Janet. THE PROGRESS OF AFRO-AMERICAN WOMEN: A SELECTED
BIBLIOGRAPHY AND RESOURCE GUIDE. Westport, CT: Greenwood Press,
1980.

Citations to over 4000 works on and by Afro-American women,
including thirty-four topical areas and subject and author
indexes. 378 pages.

37. Soltow, Martha Jane and Mary K. Wery. AMERICAN WOMEN AND THE LABOR
MOVEMENT; 1825 - 1974: AN ANNOTATED BIBLIOGRAPHY. New York, NY:
Scarecrow Press, 1977.

Includes references to books, monographs, journal articles and
government documents under eight topical subject headings. 726
pages.

38. Stineman, Ester. WOMEN'S STUDIES: A RECOMMENDED CORE BIBLIOGRAPHY.
Littleton, CO: Libraries Unlimited, 1979.

Includes selectively annotated citations to classic works in
feminist theory, movement literature and references for bibliographies, biographies and audiovisual materials. 670 pages.

39. Terris, Virginia. WOMAN IN AMERICA: A GUIDE TO INFORMATION SOURCES. Detroit, MI: Gale Research Company, 1980.

    Provides annotated references for research into the lives of American women. Includes information on general references, role, image, status, history, the women's movement, education, sociology, employment, health, mental health, sexuality, women in the arts, biographies, and autobiographies. Citations are for books, government documents, pamphlets, and periodical articles. 520 pages.

40. Tingley, Elizabeth and Donald Tingley. WOMEN AND FEMINISM IN AMERICAN HISTORY: A GUIDE TO INFORMATION SOURCES. Detroit, MI: Gale Research Company, 1981.

    Annotated bibliography of monographs, books and articles and guide to manuscript collections and biographical directories. Includes author and subject indexes. 289 pages.

41. Tinker, Irene, Michele Bo Bramsen, and Mayra Buvinic. WOMEN AND WORLD DEVELOPMENT WITH AN ANNOTATED BIBLIOGRAPHY. New York, NY: Praeger, 1976.

    Citations arranged by topical issue. Includes subject and author indexes. 382 pages.

42. Warren, Mary Anne. THE NATURE OF WOMAN; AN ENCYCLOPEDIA AND GUIDE TO THE LITERATURE. Inverness, CA: Edgepress, 1980.

    Contains 200 entries on Western philosophers and social scientists from prehistory to 1979. Extensively annotated. 700 pages.

43. White, Barbara, AMERICAN WOMEN WRITERS: AN ANNOTATED BIBLIOGRAPHY OF CRITICISM. New York, NY: Garland Publishers, 1977. 126 pages.

44. Williamson, Jane. NEW FEMINIST SCHOLARSHIP: A GUIDE TO BIBLIO-GRAPHIES. Old Westbury, NY: Feminist Press, 1979.

    Annotated citations to four hundred bibliographies relevant to research on women, including resource lists, books, and biblioographic studies appearing in scholarly journals in thirty subject areas. 144 pages.

II.
ISSUES AND PERSPECTIVES
ON THE INTEGRATION OF
WOMEN'S STUDIES

The development of the new scholarship on women has confronted educators with a wide range of issues that involve curricular, pedagogical, and institutional responses. The works listed in this section address the breadth of those issues. Citations for scholarship on the nature of Women's Studies and feminist theorizing are offered. These will be helpful in understanding the goals and points of view taken in feminist research.

Some of the works cited here discuss issues related to curricular balance and transformation. Others examine aspects of the educational experience of women in different educational settings and at different levels. Many include an analysis of the implications of recent findings on the status of women in higher education and offer recommendations for changes in teaching styles, teacher/student relationships and institutional structures. Several of these resources will be especially helpful to administrators and others in leadership roles who would like to know more about how they can be influential in establishing an organizational climate for change. This background information on Women's Studies will be valuable reading as well for educators in all disciplines.

45. Baker, Mary Anne and Catherine White Berheidi. WOMEN TODAY: A MULTIDISCIPLINARY APPROACH TO WOMEN. Monterey, CA: Brooks/Cole, 1980.

> Serves as a multidisciplinary introduction to women's studies. Focuses on women in the United States within the last twenty to thirty years. Covers the women's movement, sex role socialization, biological sex differences, women and economics, and women in politics.

46. Bowles, Gloria, and Renate Duelli-Klein, eds. THEORIES OF WOMEN'S STUDIES. London: Routledge and Kegan Paul, 1983.

Explores the nature of Women's Studies and various methodologies for conducting feminist research. Examines the value of theory. Includes a bibliography of articles on theories of Women's Studies.

47. Boxer, Marilyn. "Review Essay: For and About Women: The Theory and Practice of Women's Studies in the United States." SIGNS, 7 (1982-83), 661-695.

48. Bunch, Charlotte. "Not by Degrees." QUEST, 5, 1 (1979), 7-18.

Bunch delineates how feminist theory can be used as an analytic framework to inform the feminist movement and its educational and political goals. She discusses the link between theory and action and encourages theorizing as one means of intellectual and personal growth for women.

49. Castelli, Elizabeth. "Traditions and Transitions: Women's Studies and a Balanced Curriculum: Selected Bibliography." Los Angeles, CA: Claremont Colleges, June 1983.

Unannotated selective compilation of recent key feminist works in the liberal arts disciplines.

50. Change Magazine Editors. WOMEN ON CAMPUS: THE UNFINISHED LIBERA-TION. New Rochelle, NY: Change Magazine, 1975.

Twenty-two essays written by women scholars from diverse fields of academic study based on personal experiences in higher education.

51. Clifford, Geraldine Jonich. "'Shaking Dangerous Questions from the Crease': Gender and American Higher Education." FEMINIST ISSUES, 3 (Fall 1983), 3-62.

Constructs an historical account of women's entrance and participation in higher education. Discusses women and institutional change.

52. Conner, Daryl R. and Robert Patterson. "Building Commitment to Organizational Change." TRAINING AND DEVELOPMENT JOURNAL, 36, 4 (April 1982), 18-26 and 28-30.

Presents organizational theory on how to develop a commitment to change in institutions. Applicable to feminist concerns, although they are not specifically addressed.

53. Cruikshank, Margaret, ed. LESBIAN STUDIES, PRESENT AND FUTURE. Old Westbury, NY: Feminist Press, 1982.

    Provides essays on the personal and political aspects of the lesbian experience and on classroom issues in lesbian studies courses. Includes essays on related research. Contains an appendix of nine course syllabi.

54. Douvan, Elizabeth. "Higher Education and Feminine Socialization." NEW DIRECTIONS FOR HIGHER EDUCATION, 3 (Spring 1975), 37-50.

    Explores how gender differences resulting from socialization affect the ways in which people learn. Suggests ways colleges can be more responsive to these differences and related learning needs.

55. Dudovitz, Resa, ed. "Women in Academe." Special Issue. WOMEN'S STUDIES INTERNATIONAL FORUM, 6, 2 (1983).

    Articles focus on feminist strategies for curricular, institutional and social change in higher education.

56. Erkut, Sumra and Janice Makros. PROFESSORS AS MODELS AND MENTORS FOR COLLEGE STUDENTS. Wellesley, MA: Wellesley College Center for Research on Women, 1981.

    Examines how women and men act out the role of academic and professional mentor differently with their male and female students.

57. Froschl, Merle and Jane Williamson. FEMINIST RESOURCES FOR SCHOOLS AND COLLEGES: A GUIDE TO CURRICULAR MATERIALS. Old Westbury, NY: Feminist Press, 1978.

    See no. 17.

58. Gwinn, Donald G., "Meeting New Challenges: Creating a Climate for Change." COLLEGE AND UNIVERSITY, 57, 1 (Fall 1981), 13-25.

    Discusses needed structural and curricular changes to enhance the college and university experiences for traditional and returning women students.

59. Hall, Roberta. "The Classroom Climate: A Chilly One for Women?" PROJECT ON THE STATUS AND EDUCATION OF WOMEN. Washington, DC: Association of American Colleges, 1982.

Impressive review of the recent research studies on sexism and classroom interactions. Includes recommendations for reform, personal comments from those studied and resource list.

60. Hearn, James and Susan Olzak. "The Role of the Major Department in the Reproduction of Sexual Inequality." SOCIOLOGY OF EDUCATION, 54 (July 1981), 195-205.

Assesses the reward and support structures available for women and men within the social science disciplines at major universities.

61. HOW TO INTEGRATE WOMEN'S STUDIES INTO THE TRADITIONAL CURRICULUM. Reports from the Seventeen Curriculum Projects Represented at the Sirow Conference on Curriculum Integration, 27-30 August 1981. Princeton, NJ, 1981.

Describes strategies used by seventeen curriculum projects at various universities and colleges to integrate women's studies into the curriculum. Offers practical procedures for developing a curriculum integration program and for dealing with institutional resistance to curriculum integration.

62. Howe, Florence and Paul Lauter. THE IMPACT OF WOMEN'S STUDIES ON THE CAMPUS AND THE DISCIPLINES. Washington, DC: NIE, 1980.

63. Howe, Florence. WOMEN AND THE POWER TO CHANGE. New York, NY: McGraw Hill, 1975.

Collection of four important essays on the possibility for change in women's education and professional socialization by Adrienne Rich, Aleta Wallach, Arlie Hochschild and Florence Howe.

64. Hull, Gloria T., Patricia B. Scott, and Barbara Smith, eds. ALL THE WOMEN ARE WHITE, ALL THE BLACKS ARE MEN, BUT SOME OF US ARE BRAVE: BLACK WOMEN'S STUDIES. Old Westbury, NY: Feminist Press, 1982.

The authors discuss the invisibility of black female experience of Women's Studies and Black Studies and show the relationship between sex, race, and class oppression. Includes bibliographies and Black Women's Studies course syllabi.

65. Humm, Maggie. "Women in Higher Education: A Case Study of the School for Independent Study and the Issues for Feminism." WOMEN'S STUDIES INTERNATIONAL FORUM, 6, 1 (1983), 97-105.

Reports on the educational experience of women students in The School for Independent Study.

66. Know, Alan B. "Leadership Strategies for Meeting New Challenges: Decision Making." NEW DIRECTIONS FOR CONTINUING EDUCATION, 13 (March 1982), 3-9.

67. Langland, Elizabeth and Walter Grove, eds. A FEMINIST PERSPECTIVE IN THE ACADEMY: THE DIFFERENCE IT MAKES. Chicago, IL: University of Chicago Press, 1983.

     Nine essays by scholars from the traditional humanities and social science disciplines exploring the impact of feminism and feminist scholarship in their fields.

68. LIBERAL EDUCATION AND THE NEW SCHOLARSHIP ON WOMEN: ISSUES AND CONSTRAINTS IN INSTITUTIONAL CHANGE. Report of the Wingspread Conference, 22-24 October 1982. Washington, DC: Association of American Colleges, 1981.

     Contains essays discussing how the new scholarship on women affects curricular and institutional change. Participants were college administrators and Women's Studies scholars.

69. Makros, Janice, Sumra Erkut and Lynne Spichiger. MENTORING AND BEING MENTORED: SEX-RELATED PATTERNS AMONG COLLEGE WOMEN. Wellesley, MA: Wellesley College Center for Research on Women, 1981.

70. Marcuse, Herbert. "Marxism and Feminism." WOMEN STUDIES, 2 (1979), 279-288.

     Discusses the convergent interests of feminism and marxism and suggests that feminist theory promises to add a more radical vision of social revolution.

71. McIntosh, Margaret. "The Study of Women: Implications for Reconstructing the Liberal Arts Disciplines." FORUM FOR LIBERAL EDUCATION. 4, 1 (October 1981).

     Explores the way the introduction of women's issues within the disciplines will necessarily lead to curricular transformation.

72. Papachristou, Judith, Amy Swerdlow, and Gerda Lerner. "A Ten Year Analysis of the Women's History Program at Sarah Lawrence College." WOMEN'S STUDIES QUARTERLY, 11, 2 (Summer 1983), 19-22.

     Assesses the gains and effects of the transformation of the history program at Sarah Lawrence and looks forward to continued change.

73. Polachek, S. W. "Sex Differences in College Major." INDUSTRIAL AND LABOR RELATIONS REVIEW, 31, 4 (July 1978), 63-71.

> Reviews sex differences in the selection of college majors; 1955-1973.

74. Quest Book Committee, eds. BUILDING FEMINIST THEORY: ESSAYS FROM QUEST. New York, NY: Longman, 1981.

> Contains essays by feminists who have theorized about social change.

75. Roberts, Helen, ed. DOING FEMINIST RESEARCH. London: Routledge and Kegan Paul, 1981.

> Collection of eight articles by British feminist social scientists discussing the impact of feminism on the conceptualization of methodological and ethical issues in qualitative research.

76. Roberts, Joan I., ed. BEYOND INTELLECTUAL SEXISM. New York, NY: McKay, 1976.

> Collection of twenty essays from a wide range of scholars discussing the status of women in their discipline and prospects for the future.

77. Rubaii, Sandra. "Women's Studies at the Community College." COLLEGE ENGLISH, 37 (January 1976), 510-517.

78. "The Scholar and the Feminist III: The Search for Origins." New York, NY: Barnard College, Columbia University, 1976.

79. Scott, Nancy. RETURNING WOMEN STUDENTS: A REVIEW OF RESEARCH AND DESCRIPTIVE STUDIES. Washington, DC: National Association for Women Deans, Administrators and Counselors, 1980.

> Review of the literature describing the conditions for women who return to college later in life with recommendations for meeting their special needs.

80. "So Far, So Good - So What?: Women's Studies in the UK." Special issue. WOMEN'S STUDIES INTERNATIONAL FORUM, 6, 3 (1983).

> Collection of sixteen articles assessing the progress of Women's Studies. Issues of academic legitimacy, marginality, special student populations, feminist research and campus wide curriculum impact are discussed.

81. Solomon, Lewis. MALE AND FEMALE STUDENTS: THE QUESTION OF EQUAL OPPORTUNITY. Washington, DC: H.E.W., 1976.

82. Spender, Dale. INVISIBLE WOMEN: THE SCHOOLING SCANDAL. London: Writers and Readers Publishing Cooperative, 1982.

    Challenges the myth of equal opportunity in education by exposing the ways young women are expected to conform to male institutional expectations.

83. _____. WOMEN OF IDEAS AND WHAT MEN HAVE DONE TO THEM: FROM APHRA BEHN TO ADRIENNE RICH. London: Routledge and Kegan Paul, 1982.

    Spender examines how the intellectual contributions of 150 women have been erased from the record of knowledgemaking.

84. _____, ed. MEN'S STUDIES MODIFIED: THE IMPACT OF FEMINISM ON THE ACADEMIC DISCIPLINES. New York, NY: Pergamon, 1981.

    Discusses how a feminist perspective would change the knowledge base in the disciplines. Covers fields in the humanities, natural sciences, physical sciences, and social sciences.

85. Tidball, M. Elizabeth. "Of Men and Research: The Dominant Themes in American Higher Education Include Neither Teaching Nor Women." JOURNAL OF HIGHER EDUCATION, 47 (July 1976), 373-389.

    Concludes that colleges and universities are not supportive of women faculty or students. Male views dominate and research prestige is important. Women academics define success differently.

86. Tobias, Sheila. "Women's Studies: Its Origins, Its Organization and Its Prospects." WOMEN'S STUDIES INTERNATIONAL QUARTERLY, 1, 1 (1978), 85-98.

    Reviews status of programs. Discusses emerging theoretical approaches in literature, history, art, social science.

87. "Transforming the Traditional Curriculum." Special Issue. WOMEN'S STUDIES QUARTERLY, 10, 1 (Spring 1982), 19-33.

    A special feature including progress reports from American campuses assessing the impact of feminist scholarship on the transformation of the curriculum by Margaret McIntosh, Florence Howe, Myra Dinnerstein and others.

88. Treichler Paula A. and Chris Kram.. .. "Women's Talk in the Ivory
     Tower." COMMUNICATION QUARTERLY, 31, 2 (Spring 1983), 118-132.

          Reviews the contemporary research on university and college
          classroom interaction patterns. Concludes male patterns
          predominate and offers suggestions for teaching and research.

89. Vartulli, Sue, ed. THE PH.D EXPERIENCE: A WOMAN'S POINT OF VIEW.
     New York, NY: Praeger Publishers, 1982.

          Discusses what happens when a woman pursues a doctoral degree
          and outlines the experience of 11 women at Ohio State Uni-
          versity.

90. "Women and Education." Special Issue. OFF OUR BACKS, 12 (May 1982).

          Includes articles on Black Women's Studies, the integration of
          feminist teaching styles into the general curriculum, and
          reports by lesbian and Third World women who were fired due
          to their radical politics.

91. "Women: New Challenges, New Directions." Special Issue. HUMBOLDT
     JOURNAL OF SOCIAL RELATIONS, 10, 2 (1984).

          Assesses the effects of feminist strategies in the contempo-
          rary reform of the academic curriculum and applied social
          science research methodology.

92. "Women's Studies." Special Section. CHANGE. 14, 3 (April 1982),
     12-46.

          Includes articles that deal with the implications of feminist
          scholarship for the traditional disciplines and the development
          of a balanced curriculum.

III.
LITERARY STUDIES
AND WRITING

During the mid-1960s scholars in literature and writing did much of
the pioneer work in Women's Studies. In response to Florence Howe's now
famous question, "Where are the women?," this initial research tended
to focus on the exclusion of women from the traditional literary canon.
It suggested strategies designed to recover lost works by women poets
and authors and restore them to the curriculum. It assessed the portrayal of women in literature, the dominance of male centered themes in
literary criticism and the effects of sexist language usage. Attempts
to revise the canon and pose new thematic questions engendered discussions of new modes of inquiry and proposals for pedagogical reform
within the discipline. Research in women's literary criticism and
rhetoric thus began to take an interdisciplinary perspective and draw on
sociological, psychological, and linguistic and philosophical studies.
Conventional literary aesthetics were questioned and descriptions of
model courses and class activities in writing and literary studies were
disseminated. A currently emerging trend in the field is the development of treatises on feminist criticism and theory. This work encompas-
ses questions of research method, curriculum content and pedagogy that
will have far reaching implications for feminist scholarship within the
other liberal arts disciplines.

In this section the trends in women's scholarship within literary
studies and writing are presented. The numerous studies of particular
women writers as well as the works of women poets and authors have not
been included. Guides to these can be found within the bibliographic
studies cited in Section I. In what follows, Women in the Profession
contains reports of women's status and role in teaching and scholarship.
In the second subsection, Reconceptualizing the Discipline, representative works in feminist literary criticism, rhetoric and writing are
listed. In Thematic Studies, the citations focus on new works that are
organized around questions pertaining to women. Language and Rhetoric
contains references to works on language use and communication styles
relevant to writing and teaching. Curriculum Strategies refers the
reader to exemplary curriculum projects and cites recent treatises on
feminist pedagogy.

A. WOMEN IN THE PROFESSION

93. DeSole, Gloria and Lenore Hoffman, eds. ROCKING THE BOAT: ACA-
     DEMIC WOMEN, ACADEMIC PROCESSES. Commission on the Status of
     Women in the Profession. New York, NY: The Modern Language
     Association of America, 1981.

94. Howe, Florence and Laura Morlock. STATUS OF WOMEN IN MODERN
     LANGUAGE DEPARTMENTS: New York, NY: Publications of the
     Modern Language Association of America, 1971.

B. RECONCEPTUALIZING THE DISCIPLINE

95. Belsey, Catherine. CRITICAL PRACTICE. London: Methuen, 1980.

     A Marxist feminist reconceptualization of trends in literary
     criticism with suggestions for a new feminist approach to
     literary studies.

96. Brownstein, Rachel M. BECOMING A HEROINE: READING ABOUT WOMEN IN
     NOVELS. New York, NY: Viking Press, 1982.

     Discusses the social and psychological effects of the popular
     protrayal of women figures in literature.

97. Diamond, Arlyn. "Practicing Feminist Literary Criticism." WOMEN'S
     STUDIES INTERNATIONAL QUARTERLY, 1, 2 (1978), 149-152.

98. Donovan, Josephine, ed. FEMINIST LITERARY CRITICISM: EXPLORATIONS
     IN THEORY. Lexington, KY: University Press of Kentucky, 1975.

99. Ellman, Mary. THINKING ABOUT WOMEN. New York, NY: Harcourt, Brace
     and World, 1968.

     Early feminist work in contemporary literary theory that
     examines historical stereotypes of women writers.

100. Fetterley, Judith. THE RESISTING READER: A FEMINIST APPROACH TO
     AMERICAN FICTION. Bloomington, IN: Indiana University Press, 1978.

     Reexamines modern American literature and literary criticism
     and identifies trends that have been influenced by male bias.

101. Gallop, Jane. THE DAUGHTER'S SEDUCTION: FEMINISM AND PSYCHO-
     ANALYSIS. Ithaca, NY: Cornell University Press, 1982.

Examines the relation between feminism and the psychoanalytic theories of Jacques Lacan. Discusses such topics as reading, writing, and language.

102. Gould, Karen. "Setting Words Free: Feminist Writing in Quebec." SIGNS, 6 (Summer 1981), 617-42.

Discusses the explosion of feminist literary activity in Quebec and its contributions to feminist theatre.

103. Heilbrun, Carolyn. REINVENTING WOMANHOOD. New York, NY: Norton, 1981.

Investigates literature, folklore and mythology and analyses the problems women authors have had in presenting progressive models of female behavior and experience.

104. Jehlen, Myra. "Archimedes and the Paradox of Feminist Criticism." SIGNS, 6 (Summer 1981), 575-601.

Discusses feminist thinking as the rethinking of the assumptions underlying and organizing all our thinking, categories and terms. Argues for a feminist literary criticism that confronts fundamental axioms of the parent discipline.

105. Kahn, Coppelia and Gayle Greene, eds. FEMINIST THEORY AND CRITICISM. New York, NY: Methuen, 1984.

Collection of ten essays by feminist scholars including analyses of literary criticism, the traditional literary canons, psychoanalysis and literature, structuralist theory, marxist theory and language.

106. Kolodny, Annette. "Dancing Through the Minefield: Some Observations on the Theory, Practice and Politics of a Feminist Literary Criticism." FEMINIST STUDIES, 6 (Spring 1980), 1-25.

107. Messer-Davidow, Ellen and Joan Hartman, eds. WOMEN IN PRINT: OPPORTUNITIES FOR WOMEN'S RESEARCH IN LANGUAGE AND LITERATURE. New York, NY: Modern Language Association of America, 1982.

Assesses areas in literature and language where research is needed. Reviews kinds of scholarship that are emerging and proposes research issues and thematics for the future.

108. Rich, Adrienne. ON LIES, SECRETS AND SILENCE. New York, NY: Norton, 1979.

Explores the psychological and sociological oppression of women's creativity and expression. Analyses the institutional relationships that foster women's reluctance to speak and be heard. Makes proposals for change for students and teachers.

109. Widdowson, Peter, ed. REREADING ENGLISH. London: Methuen, 1982.

Collection of sixteen essays that discuss new trends in literary criticism. Articles by Catherine Belsey and Wendy Mulford explore feminist rereadings.

C. THEMATIC STUDIES

110. Davidson, Cathy N. and E. M. Broner, eds. THE LOST TRADITION: MOTHERS AND DAUGHTERS IN LITERATURE. New York, NY: Fredrick Ungar, 1980.

Collection of twenty-four essays by feminist scholars in the social sciences, literature and psychology analysing the nature of the mother and daughter relationship and its portrayal in literature.

111. "Feminist Critiques of Shakespeare." Special Issue. WOMEN'S STUDIES, 9, 1 (1981).

Seven articles that reassess traditional treatments of the Shakespearean plays and propose strategies for feminist rereadings.

112. Fisher, Dexter, ed. THE THIRD WOMAN: MINORITY WOMEN WRITERS IN THE UNITED STATES. Boston, MA: Houghton Mifflin, 1980.

Selections from neglected minority writers including brief biographical introductions to their work.

113. Gilbert, Sandra M. and Susan Gubar. THE MADWOMAN IN THE ATTIC: THE WOMAN WRITER AND THE NINETEENTH-CENTURY LITERARY IMAGINATION. New Haven, CT: Yale University Press, 1979.

Discussion of Jane Austen, Emily Bronte, Mary Shelly and Emily Dickenson and the extent to which the social and psychological constraints they faced as women affected their creative work.

114. Hardwick, Elizabeth. SEDUCTION AND BETRAYAL: WOMEN AND LITERATURE. New York, NY: Random House, 1975.

Collection of essays based on lectures given at Vassar and
Princeton on the fictional portrayal of women by Hawthorne,
Hardy, Ibsen, Dreiser, Richardson, Eliot and the Brontes.

115. Jacobus, Mary, ed. WOMEN WRITING AND WRITING ABOUT WOMEN.
Totowa, NJ: Barnes & Noble, 1979.

Collection of essays dealing with a wide range of women
writers and their portrayals of women.

116. Kahn, Coppelia. MAN'S ESTATE: MASCULINE IDENTITY IN SHAKESPEARE.
Berkeley, CA: University of California Press, 1981.

Using a feminist rereading of Freud and Erikson, the author
analyses the psychological archetype of male identity in the
works of Shakespeare.

117. Kennard, Jean. VICTIMS OF CONVENTION. New York, NY: Archon, 1978.

Explores the way women writers from the nineteenth through
the twentieth century have been constrained by literary and
social convention. Proposes the possibility of a convention-
less literature.

118. Lysaght, Patricia. "An Bhean Chaointe: The Supernational Women
in Irish Folklore." EIRE - IRELAND, 14 (Winter 1979), 7-29.

Traces the history of the banshee in Irish folklore.

119. Macpike, Loralee. "The Social Values of Childbirth in the
Nineteenth-Century Novel." INTERNATIONAL JOURNAL OF WOMEN'S
STUDIES, 3 (March-April 1980), 117-30.

Traces the use of childbirth as a metaphor by which women
could be judged good or evil.

120. McCaffrey, Kathleen M. "Images of Women in West African Literature
and Film: A Struggle Against Dual Colonization." INTERNATIONAL
JOURNAL OF WOMEN'S STUDIES, 3 (January-February 1980), 76-88.

Explores the West African woman's relationship to 3 major
areas of culture and society - language, her body, and work -
as reflected in recent works of Ghanian and Senegalese
literature and film.

121. Meyer, Doris and Margarite Fernandez Olnos, eds. CONTEMPORARY
WOMEN AUTHORS OF LATIN AMERICA: INTRODUCTORY ESSAYS. New York
NY: Brooklyn College Press, 1983.

Collection of twelve interpretive studies on contemporary women writers.

122. "Mothers and Daughters in Literature." Special Issue. WOMEN'S STUDIES. 6, 2 (1979).

    Several articles dealing with the writer's creative treatment of relationships between mothers and daughters. Includes a useful bibliography.

123. Newton, Judith Lowder. WOMEN, POWER AND SUBVERSION: SOCIAL STRATEGIES IN BRITISH FICTION, 1778-1860. Athens, GA: University of Georgia Press, 1981.

    Discusses the way women were characterized in British fiction during the period. Focuses particularly on women's limited exercise of power in the family and exclusion from the public sphere.

124. Pratt, Annis. ARCHETYPAL PATTERNS IN WOMEN'S FICTION. Bloomington, IN: Indiana University Press, 1982.

125. Rigney, Barbara Hill. LILITH'S DAUGHTERS: WOMEN AND RELIGION IN CONTEMPORARY FICTION. Madison, WI: University of Wisconsin Press, 1982.

    Explores the way women's religious sensibilities are characterized in contemporary fiction.

126. Showalter, Elaine. A LITERATURE OF THEIR OWN: WOMEN NOVELISTS FROM BONTE TO LESSING. Princeton, NJ: Princeton University Press, 1977.

127. Torres, Betty H. and Alberta Arthurs. "The American Eve: A New Look at American Heroines and Their Critics." INTERNATIONAL JOURNAL OF WOMEN'S STUDIES, 1, 2 (1978), 167-177.

D. LANGUAGE AND RHETORIC

128. Burke, Carolyn. "Irigaray Through the Looking Glass." FEMINIST STUDIES, 7 (Summer 1981), 255-306.

    Examines Irigaray's work and her thesis on the possibility of an analogy between female sexuality and women's language and writing.

129. Cassirer, Sidonie, ed. FEMALE STUDIES IX: TEACHING ABOUT WOMEN IN
      THE FOREIGN LANGUAGES. Old Westbury, NY: Feminist Press, 1976.

130. Hiatt, Mary P. "The Feminine Style: Theory and Fact." COLLEGE
      COMPOSITION AND COMMUNICATION, 29, 3 (1978), 222-226.

         Reviews the literature and discusses the question of the
         feminine style in the act of writing and language.

131. Klann-Delius, Gisela. "Can Women's Language Cause Changes?"
      JOURNAL OF PRAGMATICS, 4 (December 1980), 537-542.

         The author discusses the need for developing a woman's
         language but also discusses the limits of its power pointing
         to the need for political action to overcome inequality.

132. Lakoff, Robin. LANGUAGE AND WOMEN'S PLACE. New York, NY: Harper
      and Row, 1975.

         Explores the relationship between sexist language and women's
         historical social and psychological opression.

133. McConnell-Ginet, Sally, Ruth Borker, and Nelly Furman. WOMEN AND
      LANGUAGE IN LITERATURE AND SOCIETY. New York, NY: Praeger, 1980.

         Collection of twenty-one essays by anthropologists, linguists
         and literary critics exploring the effects of sexist language.

134. Silberstein, Sandra. "Bibliography: Women and Language." MICHI-
      GAN OCCASIONAL PAPERS IN WOMEN'S STUDIES. Ann Arbor, MI: Uni-
      versity of Michigan, 1980.

         Annotated bibliography of recent articles and books on the topic

135. Taylor, Sheila Ortiz. "Women in a Double-Bind: Hazards of the
      Argumentative Edge." COLLLEGE COMPOSITION AND COMMUNICATION, 29,
      4, (1978), 285-290.

         Analyses the problems associated with women's use of tra-
         ditional forms of argument.

136. Vetterling-Braggin, Mary, ed. SEXIST LANGUAGE. Totowa, NJ:
      Littlefield Adams, 1981.

         Twenty-three essays representing pro and con analyses by con-
         temporary philosophers of the feminist claim that much of
         language is sexist and that the use of such language should be
         discontinued or supplanted by the use of non-sexist language.

137. "Writing and Sexual Difference." Special Issue. CRITICAL INQUIRY, (Winter 1981).

      Collection of essays by scholars in literary criticism and linguistics exploring gender related issues in writing.

E. CURRICULUM STRATEGIES

138. COMMISSION ON SEXISM GUIDELINES FOR ENGLISH TEACHERS. Redland, CA: California Teachers of English, 1977.

139. Folsom, Jack. "Teaching About Sexism and Language in a Traditional Setting: Surmounting the Obstacles." WOMEN'S STUDIES QUARTERLY, 11, 1 (Spring 1983), 12-14.

      Discusses organization, format, teaching objectives and the design of student projects in a new course taught at Montana State University.

140. Folsom, Marcia McClintock. "Gallant Red Brick and Plain China: Teaching "A Room of One's Own." COLLEGE ENGLISH, 45, 3 (March 1983), 254-262.

141. Fry, William A. "The Changing Image of Women in Literature by American Women: A Suggested Course for the Literary Curriculum." TEACHING ENGLISH IN THE TWO YEAR COLLEGE, I (Fall 1974), 35-41.

142. _____. "Identity and Expression. A Writing Course for Women." COLLEGE ENGLISH, 32 (May 1971), 863-871.

143. Hoffman, Lenore and Deborah Rosenfelt, eds. TEACHING WOMEN'S LITERATURE FROM A REGIONAL PERSPECTIVE. New York, NY: Modern Language Association of America, 1982.

      Collection of essays describing course design, use and collection of unpublished manuscripts and diaries, and student projects associated with teaching courses in Southern women's literature and culture.

144. Jagger, Allison et al, eds. FEMINIST FRAMEWORKS. New York, NY: McGraw-Hill Book Company, 1978.

      Collection of essays by feminist scholars analysing the theoretical foundations of the liberal arts disciplines with suggestions for curricular and pedagogical reform.

145. Kolodny, Annette. "A Map for Rereading: On Gender and the Interpretation of Literary Texts." NEW LITERARY HISTORY, 11 (Spring 1980), 451-467.

A structure is proposed for rereading texts which will help men and women who do not share a literary tradition read varied styles and subjects.

146. Kurtzman, Mary. "Mainstreaming Women's Studies: Teaching composition I to Returning Women Students." OFF OUR BACKS, 12, 5 (May 1982), 22-26.

147. Lauter, Paul, ed. RECONSTRUCTING AMERICAN LITERATURE: COURSES, SYLLABI, ISSUES. Old Westbury, NY: Feminist Press, 1983.

148. Radner, Susan. "Changing Approaches to Teaching Women in Literature." FRONTIERS, 6, 2 (Spring-Summer 1981), 3-8.

149. Spann, Sylvia and M. B. Culp, eds. THEMATIC UNITS IN TEACHING ENGLISH AND THE HUMANITIES. Urbana, IL: NCTE, 1977.

Collection of teaching units including descriptions of ways to reform pedagogical practice, and equalize the treatment of males and females in literature. Provides suggestions for student projects and assignments.

IV.
SCIENCE AND TECHNOLOGY

This section contains works relevant to women's issues in science and technology. Research in this area began as a scholarly examination of the striking underrepresentation and low status of women in the scientific and technical professions. Early efforts attempted to describe the conditions for women in the traditionally male spheres of medicine, engineering and the natural and physical sciences, and confirmed the existence of inequity in graduate education, professional recognition, status and pay. More recent works sought to recover the historical contributions of women within science and technology, focused on factors contributing to women's exclusion and participation and suggested means to enhance the recruitment and retention of women. These trends continue, and the content and methods of the sciences have now begun to receive some critical attention from feminist philosophers as well. Scholarship that raises questions pertaining to scientific ethics, the nature of objectivity, traditional accounts of evolution, genetics and the treatment of sex differences is now emerging within the disciplinary literature.

In this section of the bibliography, Women in the Profession refers readers to works that chronicle the underrepresentation of women and describes present professional conditions. Reconceptualizing the Curriculum lists recent feminist works in the philosophy of science and ethical considerations of science and technology. The special issue selected for this section, Factors in Exclusion and Participation, highlights contributions to the study of professional selection and socialization, as well as analyses of social and psychological barriers to professional access and achievement. Curriculum Strategies contains citations for selected programs in career exploration and model projects to foster the retention of women in graduate programs.

A. WOMEN IN THE PROFESSION

150. Aldrich, Michelle. "Women in Science." SIGNS, 4, 1 (1978), 126-135.

> A review of the recent literature concerning the status of women in the sciences, including special problems faced in graduate training recruitment, hiring and on the job discrimination.

151. Arditti, Rita, Pat Brennan, and Steve Cavreak, eds. SCIENCE AND LIBERATION. Boston, MA: South End Press, 1980.

   Collection of articles by and about women in science, including discussions of the situation within graduate training programs and in the professions within each scientific discipline.

152. Cole, Jonathan R. FAIR SCIENCE: WOMEN IN THE SCIENTIFIC COMMUNITY. New York, NY: Free Press, 1979.

153. Eckart, Dennis R. "Microprocessors, Women and Future Employment Opportunities?" INTERNATIONAL JOURNAL OF WOMEN'S STUDIES, 5 (January-February 1982), 47-57.

154. Kreinberg, Nancy. I'M MADLY IN LOVE WITH ELECTRICITY AND OTHER COMMENTS ABOUT THEIR WORK BY WOMEN IN SCIENCE AND ENGINEERING. Berkeley, CA: University of California, Lawrence Hall of Science, 1977.

   Women in science and engineering comment about their work and their adjustments to professional life styles.

155. Menninger, Sally Ann and Clare Rose. "Women Scientists and Engineers in American Academia." INTERNATIONAL JOURNAL OF WOMEN'S STUDIES, 3 (May-June 1980), 292-299.

   Reviews the career development of women scientific professionals as well as institutional policy affecting women's professional education in American graduate schools.

156. Rossiter, M. W. WOMEN SCIENTISTS IN AMERICA: STRUGGLES AND STRATEGIES TO 1940. Baltimore: MD: Johns Hopkins University Press, 1982.

   Examines the history of women in science, tracing their participation and marginality through three periods: prior to 1880, from 1880 to 1910 and 1910 through 1940. Although the author finds increased participation, she demonstrates that women have increasingly been assigned lesser roles and have been denied recognition.

157. Strauss, Mary Jo Boehm. "Wanted: More Women in Science." AMERICAN BIOLOGY TEACHER, 40, (March 1978), 181-185.

158. "Women and Science," Special Issue. INTERNATIONAL JOURNAL OF WOMEN'S STUDIES. Connie Stark - Adamec, Guest Editor. 4 (September-October 1981).

Collection of articles by women scientists and historians that explore the experiences of women scientists and the influence of women on science.

159. "Women, Technology and Innovation," Special Issue. WOMEN'S STUDIES INTERNATIONAL FORUM, Joan Rothschild, Guest Editor. 4, 3 (1981).

This special issue includes a section on women's studies and technology.

160. Zahm, H. J. and H. J. Mozans. WOMAN IN SCIENCE. Cambridge, MA: M.I.T. Press, 1974.

An historical overview of women's contributions to science from antiquity to the early twentieth century, including biographies of women scientists. Originally published in 1913.

B. RECONCEPTUALIZING THE DISCIPLINE

161. Bleier, Ruth. "Bias in Biological and Human Science: Some Comments." SIGNS, 4, (Fall 1978), 159-162.

Critiques sociobiology.

162. Brighton Women & Science Group. ALICE THROUGH THE MICROSCOPE. London: Virago Press, 1980.

Presents an overview of science as an instrument used in the social control of women in Western society. Investigates the accessibility of science to women, barriers in the educational system in excluding women from science, problems in scientific theories, and science and the treatment of women's bodies.

163. Capra, Fritjof. THE TURNING POINT: SCIENCE, SOCIETY AND THE RISING CULTURE. New York, NY: Simon and Schuster, 1982.

Theoretical physicist writes of the connections between physics, Eastern philosophies, and social change.

164. Fee, Elizabeth. "Is Feminism a Threat to Scientific Objectivity?" INTERNATIONAL JOURNAL OF WOMEN'S STUDIES, 4 (1981), 378-392.

An exploration of the problem of objectivity in scientific research and the feminist scientist's concern to contextualizing scientific inquiry.

165. Fougen, Myra, Susan Gordon and Betty Highley. GENES AND GENDER IV: THE SECOND X AND WOMEN'S HEALTH. New York, NY: Gordian Press, 1978.

     Six articles collected from a conference on scientific approaches to women's health.

166. Haraway, Donna. "Animal Sociology and a Natural Economy of the Body Politics, Part 1: A Political Physiology of Dominance." SIGNS, 4, (Fall 1978), 21-36.

     Critiques the justification of male dominance in society often based on findings in biobehavioral sciences and explains the importance of reconceptualizing the natural and social sciences to form a dialectical understanding of social relations that is not based on domination.

167. _____. "Animal Sociology and a Natural Economy of the Body Politic, Part II: The Past as the Contested Zone: Human Nature and Theories of Production and Reproduction in Primate Behaviour Studies." SIGNS, 4, (Fall 1978), 37-60.

     Describes attempts of feminists to articulate adequate bio-social theories that eliminate the bias in existing theories of animal and human society. Questions the natural necessity of aggression, competition, and hierarchy.

168. Hubbard, Ruth. "Reflections on the Story of the Double Helix." WOMEN'S STUDIES INTERNATIONAL QUARTERLY, 2 (1979), 261-273.

169. Hubbard, Ruth and Marian Lowe, eds. GENES AND GENDER II: PITFALLS IN RESEARCH IN SEX AND GENDER. New York, NY: Gordian Press, 1979.

     Collection of seven essays on sex bias in right brain, left brain research, primatology and sociobiology.

170. Hubbard, Ruth, Mary Sue Henifin, and Barbara Fried, eds. WOMEN LOOK AT BIOLOGY LOOKING AT WOMEN: A COLLECTION OF FEMINIST CRITIQUES. Cambridge, MA: Scheckman, 1979.

     Collection of essays by women in biology exploring traditional treatments of sex and gender.

171. Keller, Evelyn Fox. "Baconian Science: A Hermaphroditic Birth." THE PHILOSOPHICAL FORUM, 11, 3 (1980), 299-308.

     Argues that the Baconian vision is less concerned with domination than recent feminist critiques have charged.

172. _____. "Feminism and Science." SIGNS, 7 (1981-82), 589-602.

Explores the male biases embedded in the foundational assumptions that guide scientific inquiry in the physical and
natural sciences and suggests that there is a feminine side
of science that has not received traditional recognition.

173. Lambert, Helen H. "Biology and Equality: A Perspective on Sex
Differences." SIGNS, 4, (Fall 1978), 97-117.

174. Lowe, Marian. "Sociobiology and Sex Differences." SIGNS, 4, (Fall
1978), 118-125.

Discusses the uncritical acceptance of the theory of sociobiology and argues that it does not meet scientific criteria.

175. Magner, Lois N. "Women and the Scientific Idiom: Textual Episodes
from Wollstonecraft, Fuller, Gilman, and Firestone." SIGNS, 4,
(Fall 1978), 61-80.

Reviews the concepts of these four feminists on science as a
body of knowledge.

176. Merchant, Carolyn. THE DEATH OF NATURE: WOMEN, ECOLOGY AND THE
SCIENTIFIC REVOLUTION. San Francisco, CA: Harper and Row, 1980.

A feminist reconceptualization of the history of science
dealing with gender, ecology and traditional definitions of
nature.

177. Mosedale, Susan Sleeth. "Science Corrupted: Victorian Biologists
Consider 'The Woman Question.'" JOURNAL OF THE HISTORY OF BIOLOGY,
11, 1 (1978), 1-56.

Explains how prominent Victorian era biologists used their
science to confirm their social attitudes toward women.

178. Reed, Evelyn. SEXISM AND SCIENCE. New York, NY: Pathfinder Press,
1978.

Collection of essays by and about women in science. Includes
discussions of sociobiology, matriarchy and evolutionary theory.

179. Rothschild, Joan A. "A Feminist Perspective on Technology and the
Future." WOMEN'S STUDIES INTERNATIONAL QUARTERLY, 4, 1 (1981),
65-74.

Explores the anti-humanistic tendencies of technological expansion and argues from a feminist perspective for alternative visions of the future.

180. Sayers, Janet. BIOLOGICAL POLITICS: FEMINIST AND ANTIFEMINIST PERSPECTIVES, New York, NY: Methuen, 1982.

Examines how biology has been used to explain sexual inequality. Compares feminist and antifeminist biological theories.

181. Tanner, Nancy Makepeace. ON BECOMING HUMAN. New York, NY: Cambridge University Press, 1981.

Explores woman's role in human evolution.

182. Tobach, Ethel and Betty Rosoff, eds. GENES AND GENDER: I. New York, NY: Gordian Press, 1978.

Collection of articles by and about women in the biological sciences dealing with the scientific treatment of women as objects.

183. _____. GENES AND GENDER III: GENETIC DETERMINATION AND CHILDREN. New York, NY: Gordian Press, 1980.

Collection of articles dealing with the issue by feminist scholars in the biological and medical sciences.

184. Zihlman, Adrienne L. "Women and Evolution, Part II: Subsistence and Social Organization among Early Homonids." SIGNS, 4, (Fall 1978), 4-20.

Reconstructs evolutionary theory by illuminating the critical role of human females in the success of the species.

C. SPECIAL ISSUE:
FACTORS IN EXCLUSION AND PARTICIPATION

185. Arditti, Rita. "Feminism and Science," in SCIENCE AND LIBERATION, Rita Arditti et al., eds. Boston, MA: South End Press, 1980, 350-368.

Provides a comprehensive review of the status and prospects of women in science and assesses the significance of feminist critiques of the scientific disciplines.

186. Arnold, Lois. "Florence Bascom and the Exclusion of Women from Earth Science Curriculum Materials." JOURNAL OF GEOLOGICAL EDUCA-TION, 23 (September 1975), 110-113.

     Analyses discrimination in excerpts from current earth science curriculum materials. Comments on important contribution of female earth scientist, Florence Bascom.

187. Briscoe, Ann and Sheila Pfafflin, eds. EXPANDING THE ROLE OF WOMEN IN THE SCIENCES. New York, NY: New York Academy of Science, 1979.

188. Chepelinsky, Ana Berta, et al. "Women in Chemistry,": in SCIENCE AND LIBERATION, Rita Arditti et al., eds. Boston, MA: South End Press 1980, 257-266.

     Offers a discussion and overview of the obstacles facing women in chemistry.

189. Fausto-Sterling, Ann. "Women and Science." WOMEN'S STUDIES INTER-NATIONAL QUARTERLY, 4, 1 (1981).

     Discusses the issue of differences in male and female approaches to science, the 'math filter' that works against women's pursuit of science in college and the social relations that tend to exclude women within the scientific professions.

190. Goldman, Roy D., and Barbara N. Hewitt. "The Scholastic Aptitude Test 'Explains' Why College Men Major in Science More often than College Women." JOURNAL OF COUNSELING PSYCHOLOGY, 23, 1 (January 1976), 50-55.

     Introduces the idea of a 'math filter' which discourages young women from continuing in science in college and university.

191. Hornig, Lili S. "Scientific Sexism." ANNALS OF NEW YORK ACADEMY OF SCIENCES, (1979), 125-133.

     Explores the way in which the professional norms within the sciences disadvantage women.

192. Humphreys, S. M., ed. WOMEN AND MINORITIES IN SCIENCE: STRATEGIES FOR INCREASING PARTICIPATION. Boulder, CO: Westview, 1982.

193. Keller, Evelyn Fox. "The Anomaly of a Woman in Physics," in WORK-ING IT OUT, Sara Ruddick and Pamela Daniels, eds. New York, NY: Pantheon, 1977, 77-91.

194. _____. A FEELING FOR THE ORGANISM: THE LIFE AND WORK OF BARBARA McCLINTOCK. San Francisco, CA: W. H. Freeman, 1983.

A biographical account of the geneticist McClintock and exploration of her identity as scientist and woman.

195. Martin, Ben and John Irvine. "Women in Science - The Astronomical Brain Drain." WOMEN'S STUDIES INTERNATIONAL FORUM, 5, 1 (1982), 41-68.

Career patterns of women in astronomy are explored.

196. O'Donnell, JoAnne and Dale Anderson. "Decision Factors Among Women Talented in Math and Science." COLLEGE STUDENT JOURNAL, 11, 2 (Summer 1977).

197. Sanderson, Marie. "Mary Somerville: Her Work in Physical Geography." GEOGRAPHICAL REVIEW, 64, 3 (1974), 410-420.

198. Sayres, Anne. ROSALIND FRANKLIN AND DNA. New York, NY: Norton, 1975.

Chronicles the historical neglect of Franklin and the discrimination she faced within the profession.

199. Trecker, Janice L. "Sex, Science and Education." AMERICAN QUARTERLY, 26 (October 1974), 352-66.

Describes the formulation of plans for women's education by conservative scientists in the 19th century that were intended to prepare women for motherhood and prevent them from challenging men intellectually.

D.   CURRICULUM STRATEGIES

200. Alic, Margaret. "The History of Women in Science: A Woman Studies Course." WOMEN'S STUDIES INTERNATIONAL FORUM, 5, 1 (1982), 75-81.

201. Chew, Martha. "A Survival Course for Women Entering a Male Dominated Profession: Women's Studies at the Massachusetts College and Allied Health Sciences." WOMEN'S STUDIES QUARTERLY, 10 (Summer 82), 19-21.

202. HYPATIA'S SISTERS: BIOGRAPHIES OF WOMEN SCIENTISTS PAST AND PRESENT. Seattle, WA: Feminists Northwest, 1976.

Collection of short biographies from 3000 BC to the present compiled by a Women in Science class at the University of Washington.

203. Kamel, Rose. "Women's Studies and the Professional School: A Contradiction in Terms?" COLLEGE ENGLISH, 44, 7 (November 1982), 685-691.

Describes a course in women's literature designed for students in the applied sciences.

204. Krammer, Ann E., Cherlyn S. Granrose, and Jan B. Sloan, eds. SCIENCE, SEX AND SOCIETY. Newton, MA: Educational Development Center, 1979.

Collection of articles and resource listings appropriate for introductory courses in Women and Science.

205. Lantz, Alma. REENTRY PROGRAMS FOR FEMALE SCIENTISTS. New York, NY: Praeger, 1980.

Discusses the progress made in twenty-one National Science Foundation sponsored projects at American colleges and universities to aid women's reentry in science and related fields. Examines special needs of returning women students in science.

206. LeBold, William K. PUTTING IT ALL TOGETHER: A MODEL PROGRAM FOR WOMEN ENTERING ENGINEERING. Washington, DC: Women's Educational Equity Act Program, US Dept. of Education, 1983.

Describes a university wide program developed at Purdue through funds from the Women's Educational Equity Act.

207. Lee, David R. "Feminist Approaches in Teaching Geography." JOURNAL OF GEOGRAPHY, 77, (September-October 1978), 180-183.

Describes feminist teaching strategies in geography and student interest in subject matter.

208. Smith, Walter S. and Kala M. Stroup. SCIENCE CAREER EXPLORATION FOR WOMEN. Washington, DC: National Science Teachers Association, 1978.

Presents six modules exploring careers in science.

209. Wilkinson, Nancy Lee. "A Report on the 'Geographical Perspectives on Women Seminar' at the University of Oregon." JOURNAL OF GEOGRAPHY, 77, (September-October 1978), 172-174.

Describes the development and content of a college research seminar about women and geography.

210. Zinn, Mary F. "Women in Science: Why Not? Two Modules." JOURNAL OF COLLEGE SCIENCE TEACHING, 6, (January 1977), 143-148.

Presents two modules developed at Oberlin College to foster women's professional interest in science.

V.
QUANTITATIVE REASONING

Most of the research on women and mathematics has focused on factors affecting the achievement of women in the field. Researchers
have examined the effects of sex-role socialization on sex differences
in mathematics learning. Scholars have also sought to explicate the
sources of women's math anxiety and avoidance and have developed curriculum, special teaching methods, workshops and advisement practices to
respond to the problem. This issue is an important equity concern.
Women's continued avoidance of math as a product of traditional sex-role
socialization, and schooling practices that perpectuate that socialization, act as a filter that bars large numbers of women from entering
the increasing number of highly paid jobs that are concentrated in
technical and scientific fields. Within scholarhip on mathematics and
women, less attention has been given to how quantitative research itself
must be examined for sex bias or to developing quantitative research
designs with the complexity necessary for exploring research on women.
Scholarly work on these issues is just beginning to emerge and examples
are listed below.

Women in the Profession, the first subsection of citations that
follows, contains references to works that describe both women's underrepresentation and their achievement within the field. In Reconceptualizing the Discipline the majority of studies cited focus on the application of particular forms of quantitative research design to the investigation of women's issues. Fewer studies exist giving specific attention
to methodological questions and research design, but representative works
are included here. Women and Quantitative Reason contains references
to the extensive research concerning women's math anxiety and avoidance
and analyses of the cultural and institutional factors that influence the
development of women's quantitative reasoning skills. Concluding entries
in Curriculum Strategies provide information on intervention programs
designed to improve recruitment, advisement, curriculum, and pedagogy in
mathematics education.

A. WOMEN IN THE PROFESSION

211. Hewitt, Gloria C. THE STATUS OF WOMEN IN MATHEMATICS. New York,
      NY: Academy of Science, 1978.

> Discusses changes in the role of women mathematicians during
> the 1970s, textbook changes, professional organization changes,
> and the increase of women earning mathematics degrees. Also
> discusses areas where little progress has been made.

212. Kimberling, Clark. "Emmy Noether, Greatest Woman Mathematician."
      MATHEMATICS TEACHER, 75 (March 1982), 246-249.

> Presents a brief history of Amalie Emmy Noether and discusses
> her contributions to mathematics and physics. Highlights her
> work in the development of modern algebra.

213. Perl, Teri. MATH EQUALS: BIOGRAPHIES OF WOMEN MATHEMATICIANS AND
      RELATED ACTIVITIES. Menlo Park, CA: Addison-Wesley, 1978.

> Presents biographies of 10 women mathematicians and examines
> social issues related to the success of women in the field.
> Appendices provide challenging mathematical problems with
> straightforward solutions to encourage self-confidence in math.

214. Rappaport, Karen D. REDISCOVERING WOMEN MATHEMATICIANS. 1978. ERIC
      ED 160 444.

> Describes the lives and mathematical contributions of seven
> famous women mathematicians: Hypatia, Maria Agnese, Sophie
> Germain, Mary Sommerville, Augusta Lovelace, Sofya Kovalevsky
> and Emmy Noether.

215. _____. "Rediscovering Women Mathematicians." MATYC
      JOURNAL, 13, 1, 1979.

> Reviews the lives of 3 women mathematicians; Hypatia, Maria
> Gaetana Agnesi, and Sophie Germain.

B. RECONCEPTUALIZING THE DISCIPLINE

216. Confrey, Jere. "An Examination of Female High School Students'
      Conceptions of Mathematics." Paper presented at the Annual Meet-
      ing of the American Educational Research Association, New Orleans,
      April 1984.

Examines the conceptions of mathematics held by generally able but mathematically weak high school women. Suggests how a constructivist perspective could enable young women to deal more effectively with mathematics.

217. Fine-Davis, Margaret. "Personality Correlates of Attitudes Toward the Role and Status of Women in Ireland." JOURNAL OF PERSONALITY, 47 (September 1979), 379-96.

Factor analysis, analysis of variance, and path analysis used to examine the possible relationships between personality and related social-psychological characteristics and attitudes toward sex-roles and issues relevant to the status of women. Useful model for applying quantitative research methods to the analysis of feminist issues.

218. Henderson, Jule, John Biere, and Ross Hartsough. "Sexism and Sex-Role in Letters of Recommendation to Graduate Training in Psychology." CANADIAN PSYCHOLOGIST, 21 (April 1980), 75-80.

Multivariate analysis, discriminant function analysis, and uni-variate analysis of variance. Helpful example of quantitative research design for the analysis of feminist issues.

219. Jayarantine, Toby Epstein. "The Value of Quantitative Methodology for Feminist Research." In THEORIES OF WOMEN'S STUDIES. Eds. Gloria Bowles and Renate Duelli Klein. Boston: Routledge and Kegan Paul, 1983.

Discusses feminist criticism of quantitative research methodology and strategies for overcoming its deficiencies.

220. Peay, Marilyn Y. "Use of the Sex Variable in Social Psychological Research." AUSTRALIAN PSYCHOLOGIST, 11, 2, (July 1976), 139-46.

Reviews the use of the sex variable in journal articles and classic studies and concludes that it is more often neglected in "classic" studies than in recent journal articles.

221. Rabkin, Judith Godwin. "The Epidemiology of Forcible Rape." AMERICAN JOURNAL OF ORTHOPSYCHIATRY, 49 (October 1979), 634-47.

Problems of measurement of the incidence of rape are considered, and empirical findings are summarized. Findings are discussed in the framework of blame models and their implications for treatment and prevention.

222. The "Motherhood Mandate." PSYCHOLOGY OF WOMEN QUARTERLY, 4, 1 (Fall 1979).

The assumption that motherhood is central to women's identity is examined in regard to its influence on models and methods of research in the psychology of women. Discusses complexities of research methodology that should be attended to.

223. Vandanoff, Patricia. "Perceived Job Characteristics and Job Satisfaction among Men and Women." PSYCHOLOGY OF WOMEN QUARTERLY, 5 (Winter 1980), 1977-85.

Uses zero-order correlation and multiple regression analysis. Example of the use of quantitative research methodology for analyzing feminist issues.

C. SPECIAL ISSUE: WOMEN AND QUANTITATIVE REASON

224. Armstrong, Jane and Stuart Kahl. AN OVERVIEW OF FACTORS AFFECTING WOMEN'S PARTICIPATION IN MATHEMATICS. Denver, CO: National Assessment of Educational Progress, 1979.

225. Donady, Bonnie, Stanley Kogelman, and Sheila Tobias. "Math Anxiety and Female Mental Health: Some Unexpected Links." In THE EVOLVING FEMALE: WOMEN IN PSYCHOSOCIAL CONTEXT. Carol Landau Hackerman, ed. New York, NY: Human Sciences Press, 1980, 325-346.

Discusses counseling treatments to alleviate math anxiety.

226. Fennema, Elizabeth, ed. MATHEMATICS LEARNING: WHAT RESEARCH SAYS ABOUT SEX DIFFERENCES. Columbus, OH: ERIC Information Analysis Center for Scientific, Mathematical and Environmental Education, 1975. ED 128 195.

Elizabeth Fennema, one of the first researchers on women and mathematics edited this collection of 4 papers, originally given at a symposium on sex differences and mathematics learning.

227. _____, and Carpenter, T. "Sex-related Differences in Mathematics: Results from the National Assessment." THE MATHEMATICS TEACHER, 74, 7 (1981), 554-559.

228. Fox, Lynn H. THE PROBLEM OF WOMEN AND MATHEMATICS: A REPORT TO THE FORD FOUNDATION. New York, NY: The Ford Foundation, 1981.

Explores issues related to women in mathematics and sex difference in mathematics education. Contains bibliograpy.

229. _____. et al, eds. WOMEN AND THE MATHEMATICAL MYSTIQUE.
Baltimore, MD: Johns Hopkins University Press, 1980.

Presents ten research studies by educators, psycholgists, and
sociologists on the obstacles women experience in pursuing a
career in mathematics. Findings indicate that negative
attitudes, socioenvironmental factors, and differential
encouragement act as barriers to the achievement of women in
mathematics.

230. Hendel, Darwin D. "Experiential and Affective Correlates of Math
Anxiety in Adult Women." PSYCHOLOGY OF WOMEN QUARTERLY, 5, 2
(Winter 1980), 219-30.

Research investigating correlates of math anxiety in women.

231. Sherman, Julia. "Continuing in Mathematics: A Longitudinal Study
of the Attitudes of High School Girls." PSYCHOLOGY OF WOMEN
QUARTERLY, 7, 2 (Winter 1982), 132-140.

232. Sherman, Julia A. "Mathematics the Critical Filter: A Look at Some
Residues." PSYCHOLOGY OF WOMEN QUARTERLY, 6 (Summer 1982),
428-44.

Interviews of female students regarding attitudes toward sex
role and mathematics. Results indicate continued contradiction
between the socialization of girls and math achievement.

233. Starr, Barbara Schaap. "Sex Difference Among Personality Correlates
of Mathematical Ability in High School Seniors." PSYCHOLOGY OF
WOMEN QUARTERLY, 4 (Winter 1979), 212-20.

Examines sex differences in personality correlates of mathematical ability. For females only, internal locus of control
and self-esteem were correlates of mathematical ability and
were seen as facilitators of female mathematical functioning.

234. Tobias, Sheila. OVERCOMING MATH ANXIETY. New York: Wm. Norton,
1978.

Explores reasons for fear of mathematics, especially among
women, and how this restricts subsequent career choices.
Encourages and identifies ways to overcome it.

D.   CURRICULUM STRATEGIES

235.   Blumb, L. and S. Givant.   "Increasing the Participation of Women in Fields that Use Mathematics." THE AMERICAN MATHEMATICAL MONTHLY, 87, 10 (1980), 785-793.

Describes a mathematics program for undergraduate women at Mills College emphasizing use of peer instruction.

236.   Fennema, Elizabeth, et al.   "Increasing Women's Participation in Mathematics: An Intervention Study." JOURNAL OF RESEARCH IN MATHEMATICS EDUCATION,12 (1981), 3-14.

Describes the use of a successful videotape workshop series, "Multiplying Options and Subtracting Bias," to encourage young women, teachers, peers, and parents to recognize the importance of continued study in mathematics.

237.   Fox, Lynn H.   "Women and the Career Relevance of Mathematics and Science." SCHOOL SCIENCE AND MATHEMATICS, 76 (April 1976), 347-53.

Argues that it is important that teachers and counselors encourage girls to prepare in these fields. Describes some special courses planned to attract girls. Includes a bibliography.

238.   Greenberg, Gilda M.   "Enlarging the Career Aspirations of Women Students by Alleviating Math and Science Anxiety." Paper presented at the Great Lakes Women's Studies Association "The Greening of Women's Studies: A Regional Conference on Feminist Education in all Settings." Northeastern Illinois University, Chicago, IL. January 20-21, 1978.

Outline and evaluation of a six-week workshop for women aimed at exploring new perspectives in careers and at increasing self-confidence in mathematical skills considered appropriate for careers in science and technology.

239.   Kaseberg, A., N. Kreinberg, and D. Downie. USE EQUALS TO PROMOTE THE PARTICIPATION OF WOMEN IN MATHEMATICS. Berkeley, CA: University of California Press, 1980.

Describes the Equals Program and offers teachers ideas for the classroom. Activities are provided to heighten awareness of young women concerning the importance of mathematics.

240. MacDonald, Carolyn T. "Introductory Mathematics and the Adult Woman Student." TWO-YEAR COLLEGE MATHEMATICS JOURNAL, 9, 3 (June 1978), 158-61.

Discusses ways to enhance the mathematics learning opportunities of the woman who is older than the traditional 18 year old undergraduate.

241. Pines, Sylvia F. "A Procedure for Predicting Underachievement in Mathematics among Female College Students." EDUCATIONAL AND PSYCHOLOGICAL MEASUREMENT, 41 (Winter 1981), 1137-1146.

Discusses a method for identifying those females who are predicted to fall substantially below their male counterparts in mathematical participation and performance so that intervention procedures can be made available to them early in their college education.

242. Skolnick, Joan, Carol Langbort, and Lucille Day. HOW TO ENCOURAGE GIRLS IN MATH AND SCIENCE: STRATEGIES FOR PARENTS AND EDUCATORS. Englewood Cliffs, NJ: Prentice-Hall, 1982.

Examines the effects of sex-role socialization on the development of skills and confidence in math and science. Provides suggestions for teaching these subjects to girls. Useful for teacher preparation programs for math educators.

243. Wolf, Mary L. "Anxiety and Stereotyped Beliefs about Statistics." EVALUATION AND THE HEALTH PROFESSIONS, 1, 4 (December 1978).

Discusses math anxiety and its implications for course redesign in statistics.

VI.
HISTORICAL PERSPECTIVES

During the last fifteen years an enormous number of works on women in history have been published. The great majority have sought to integrate the study of women within the curriculum and establish the legitimacy of scholarship on women's experiences and contributions. Several biographies of women in history began to appear in the early 1960s, followed by thematic studies of women in particular cultural contexts and eras. Important critical works that began to emerge in the late 1960s stressed women's unwarranted marginality in historical literature and the discipline's selective concern with the public spheres of politics, war, industry and labor. The historian Gerda Lerner and others called for history that might be "seen through the eyes of women" which, Lerner argued, "would mean documenting all of history."

Recent reconceptualist efforts in women's history have attempted to apply Lerner's thesis. The amount of scholarship of special relevance to women in social history, the history of the family, child rearing and education has dramatically increased. New research questions, critiques of traditional research methodologies and newly developed curricular materials have begun to have a significant impact on the discipline.

In this section of the bibliography works documenting the status and condition of women as teachers of history can be found in Women in the Profession. Reconceptualizing the Curriculum includes scholarship on women's exclusion and marginality, critiques of the traditionally conceived private-sphere/public-sphere dichotomy, and proposals for incorporating the study of women within the discipline. Works on individual female figures in history have not been included here. Guides to such works can be found among the bibliographic studies listed in Section I. Thematic Studies contains representative works that survey ancient to modern periods and particular geographical world areas. Entries on North American women are more numerous in this subsection and include references to specialized studies of women's experience in the American Southwest, New England, the South and the cities, as well as research on American women and the family, politics, slavery, emancipation and education. Curriculum Strategies includes citations to representative programs that have sought to integrate the study of women within the curriculum. Proposals for student projects in oral history and research involving unpublished diaries and letters are also presented.

A. WOMEN IN THE PROFESSION

244. COMMITTEE ON WOMEN HISTORIANS 1980 SUMMARY REPORT. Washington,
      DC: American Historical Association, February 1981.

245. Committee on Women Historians. A SURVIVAL MANUAL FOR WOMEN (AND
      OTHER) HISTORIANS. Washington, DC: American Historical Associa-
      tion, 1982.

           Reviews the status of women in the profession and explores
           the unwritten rules for success in the academy.

246. Davis, Natalie Zemon. "Gender and Genre: Women as Historical,
      Writers, 1400-1820." In BEYOND THEIR SEX: LEARNED WOMEN OF THE
      EUROPEAN PAST. Ed. Patricia H. Labalme. New York, NY: New York
      University Press, 1980, 153-182.

247. Sklar, Kathryn Kish. "American Female Historians in Context, 1770-
      1930." FEMINIST STUDIES, 3, 1-2 (1977), 171-184.

B. RECONCEPTUALIZING THE DISCIPLINE

248. Bridenthal, Renate and Claudia Koonz. "Introduction." In BECOMING
      VISIBLE: WOMEN IN EUROPEAN HISTORY. Renate Bridenthal and Claudia
      Koonz, eds. Boston, MA: Houghton Mifflin, 1977, 1-10.

           The authors propose a feminist historiography to challenge tra-
           ditional periodization of history.

249. Carroll, Berenice A., ed. LIBERATING WOMAN'S HISTORY: THEORETICAL
      AND CRITICAL ESSAYS. Urbana, IL: University of Illinois Press,
      1975.

           Anthology of articles by feminist historians and social
           scientists covering method, content and pedagogical issues.

250. Degler, Carl N. "What the Woman's Movement Has Done to American
      History." SOUNDINGS, 64 (1981), 403-421.

           The author contends that feminist research has caused a re-
           thinking of traditional themes and issues in American history
           and has reemphasized the need for work in social history.

251. Eicher, Magrit and Carol Ann Nelson. "History and Historiography:
      The Treatment in American Histories of Significant Events Concern-
      ing the Status of Women." HISTORIAN, 40, 2 (1977), 1-15.

252. Evans, Richard J. "Women's History: The Limits of Reclamation."
     SOCIAL HISTORY (Great Britain), 5, 2 (1980), 273-281.

     Criticizes the approach to women's history which takes on the
     character of an act of reclamation and also criticizes the
     biographical approach.

253. Evans, Sara. "Visions of Woman-Centered History." SOCIAL POLICY,
     12 (Spring 1982), 46-49.

     Explores three methodological approaches to doing research in
     women's history and argues for an approach that affirms
     women's contributions as well as recognizes the historical
     reality of oppression.

254. Janssen-Jurreit, Marielouise. SEXISM: THE MALE MONOPOLY ON HISTORY
     AND THOUGHT. New York, NY: Farrar, Strauss & Giroux, 1982.

     Critiques all aspects of patriarchal society and the
     conceptualizations of history, culture and economics
     dominated by a male perspective.

255. Jensen, Joan and Beverly Baca. "Family History and Oral History."
     FRONTIERS, 2, 2 (1977), 93-98.

     Argues that oral history and explorations of family histories
     enrich the scholar's understanding of the socio-historical
     context.

256. Johannson, Sheila Ryan. "'Herstory' as History: A New Field or
     Another Fad?" In LIBERATING WOMEN'S HISTORY. Berenice A. Carroll.
     ed. Champaign, IL: University of Illinois Press, 1976, 400-430.

     Discusses methodological changes needed to develop women's
     history. Emphasis on the relationship between the lives and
     social roles of women, and the nature of social change.

257. Keddie, Nikki R. "Problems in the Study of Middle Eastern Women."
     INTERNATIONAL JOURNAL OF MIDDLE EAST STUDIES (Great Britain), 10, 2
     (1979), 225-240.

     Examines some of the problems hindering the study of women's
     history in the Middle East.

258. Kinnear, Mary. DAUGHTERS OF TIME: WOMEN IN THE WESTERN TRADITION.
     Ann Arbor, MI: University of Michigan Press, 1982.

259. Kolodny, Annette. THE LAND BEFORE HER: FANTASY AND EXPERIENCE OF
THE AMERICAN FRONTIERS: 1630-1860. Chapel Hill, NC: University
of North Carolina Press, 1982.

> The author draws on literature and unpublished diaries of the
> era to create a social history of the Western experience.
> Argues that a distinctively feminized view of frontier life,
> which has been ignored in traditional histories, was an
> important force in the shaping of the Western experience.

260. Ladner, Joyce A. "Racism and Tradition: Black Womanhood in Historical Perspective." In LIBERATING WOMEN'S HISTORY. Berenice
A. Carroll. Champaign, IL: University of Illinois Press, 1976,
179-193.

> Critiques past historiography that compares the black family
> to middle-class whites. Asserts that to understand the posi-
> tion of black women in today's society, analyses of family life
> in pre-colonial African cultures and the structural effects of
> slavery are necessary.

261. Lerner, Gerda. THE MAJORITY FINDS ITS PAST: PLACING WOMEN IN
HISTORY. New York, NY: Oxford University Press, 1979.

> Lerner argues that no single methodology and conceptual frame-
> work can organize the historical experience of all types of
> women. A new history is essential, that is equally
> concerned with men, women and the establishment and passing of
> patriarchy.

262. Lougee, Carolyn C. "Modern European History: A Review Essay."
SIGNS, 2, 3 (1977), 628-650.

> Discusses approaches to women's history and methodological
> strategies which both link women's history to and differentiate
> it from the mainstream of historical writing. Discusses areas
> needing further exploration.

263. Moore, Kathryn M. "Towards a Synthesis of Organizational Theory
and Historical Analysis: The Case of Academic Women." REVIEW
OF HIGHER EDUCATION, 5 (Summer 1982), 213-223.

> Suggests integrating social theory and historical analysis
> in order to examine the experiences of women within formal
> institutional structures. Explores the history of academic
> women in the nineteenth century using this framework.

264. Morantz, Regina Markell. "The Perils of Feminist History."
JOURNAL OF INTERDISCIPLINARY HISTORY, 4, 4 (1974), 649-660.

Cautions about polemics in historical research, with specific reference to writing on 19th century medical therapeutics.

265. Riemer, Eleanor S. and John C. Fout. "Women's History: Recent Journal Articles." TRENDS IN HISTORY, 1, 1 (1979), 3-22.

Discusses articles which appeared in US and European periodical literature in 1978 on major trends in the study of women's history: sexuality, the family, women and war, attitudes toward women, education, and immigrants.

266. Rowbotham, Sheila. HIDDEN FROM HISTORY: REDISCOVERING WOMEN IN HISTORY FROM THE SEVENTEENTH CENTURY TO THE PRESENT. New York, NY: Pantheon, 1975.

Discusses women's role and status as well as response to the agricultural, industrial, French, American and Russian revolutions from a feminist-socialist perspective. Argues that women's social and political forms of activism have been ignored or undervalued in traditional history.

267. Shoub, Myra. "Jewish Women's History: Development of a Critical Methodology." CONSERVATIVE JUDAISM, 35 (Winter 1982), 33-46.

268. Smith, Hilda. "Feminism and the Methodology of Women's History." In LIBERATING WOMEN'S HISTORY, Berenice A. Caroll, ed. Champaign, IL: University of Illinois Press, 1976, 369-384.

Argues that women's history must be viewed from a feminist perspective that considers women as a distinct sociological group.

269. Steans, Peter N. "Old Women: Some Historical Observations." JOURNAL OF FAMILY HISTORY, 5, 1 (1980), 44-57.

Argues that old women deserve more attention by family historians and demographers because of their unique social roles.

270. Vann, Richard T. "Toward a New Lifestyle: Women in Preindustrial Capitalism." In BECOMING VISIBLE: WOMEN IN EUROPEAN HISTORY. Renate Bridenthal and Claudia Koonz, ed. Boston, MA: Houghton Mifflin, 1977, 192-216.

Describes the lives of "ordinary women living their everyday lives" in Europe from the Reformation of the 16th century to the Industrial Revolution of 18th century England.

271. "Women's Oral History Two," Special Issue. FRONTIERS, 7, 1 (1983).

    Over twenty-five articles discussing theory, method, pedagogy and recent research findings. Includes a selective bibliography, resource guide to regional projects and directory of collections.

C. THEMATIC STUDIES

272. Angell, Susan, Jacquelyn Down Hall and Candace Waid, eds. "Generations: Women in the South." Special Issue. SOUTHERN EXPOSURE, 4 (Winter 1977).

    Collection of articles discussing new research methodologies in feminist historical research applied to work on women in the American south.

273. Aptheker, Bettina. WOMEN'S LEGACY: ESSAYS ON RACE, SEX AND CLASS IN AMERICAN HISTORY. Amherst, MA: University of Massachusetts Press, 1982.

274. Badran, Margot Farranto. "Middle East and North Africa: Women." TRENDS IN HISTORY, 1, 1 (1979), 123-129.

    Reviews current research on women in the Middle East and Africa, discussing the particular effects of their religious and cultural traditions on their societal status and role.

275. Bainton, Roland Herbert. WOMEN OF THE REFORMATION, FROM SPAIN TO SCANDINAVIA. Minneapolis, MN: Augsburg, 1977.

276. Baxandall, Rosalyn, et al. AMERICA'S WORKING WOMEN: A DOCUMENTARY HISTORY, 1600 TO THE PRESENT. New York, NY: Random House, 1976.

277. Bekin, Carol R. and Clara M. Lovett, eds. WOMEN, WAR AND REVOLUTION. New York, NY: Holmes and Meier, 1980.

    Collection of essays discussing women's innovative actions in response to revolutionary and wartime situations during the French, American, Russian, Chinese and Cuban revolutions.

278. Branca, Patricia. "A New Perspective on Women's Work: A Comparative Typology." JOURNAL OF SOCIAL HISTORY, 9, 2 (1975), 129-153.

    Discusses the issue of women's work in the domestic and public spheres and investigates the way in which women's work has been defined and valued within various cultural contexts.

279. Bridenthal, Renate and Claudia Koonz, eds. BECOMING VISIBLE: WOMEN
     IN EUROPEAN HISTORY. Boston, MA: Houghton Mifflin, 1977.

     Collection of essays by feminist scholars reassessing the issues
     and themes relevant to women and social history.

280. Buhle, Mari Jo. WOMEN AND AMERICAN SOCIALISM. Champaign, IL:
     University of Illinois Press, 1983.

     Discusses the interconnections between the nineteenth-century
     movement for women's rights and the development of the women's
     socialist movement in the United States. Explores the contri-
     butions of radical women immigrants at the turn of the century
     and conflicts within the socialist and feminist movement.

281. Burstyn, Joan. VICTORIAN EDUCATION AND THE IDEAL OF WOMANHOOD. New
     York, NY: Barnes and Noble, 1980.

     Explores the move toward higher education for women in
     nineteenth century England and the conflicts experienced
     by educated women facing a socially dysfunctional gender
     based ideal of their proper role in society.

282. Cott, Nancy F. THE BONDS OF WOMANHOOD: "WOMAN'S SPHERE" IN NEW
     ENGLAND, 1780-1835. New Haven and London: Yale University Press,
     1977.

     Explores the experiences of middle class New England women
     and cultural definitions of women's sphere. Focuses on
     five areas of importance; work, domesticity, education,
     religion and sisterhood.

283. Courtney, Barbara. "Lives and Letters - Oh Pioneers." MASSA-
     CHUSETTS REVIEW, 18 (1977), 227-248.

284. Douglas, Ann. THE FEMINIZATION OF AMERICAN CULTURE. New York, NY:
     Avon Books, 1977.

     Discusses the historical and societal roots of the sentimental-
     ization of gender distinctions and the origins of mass culture.

285. Engel, Barbara Alpern and Clifford N. Rosenthal, eds. FIVE
     SISTERS: WOMEN AGAINST THE TSAR. New York, NY: Knopf, 1977.

286. Flexner, Eleanor. CENTURY OF STRUGGLE: THE WOMAN'S RIGHTS MOVEMENT
     IN THE UNITED STATES. Cambridge, MA: Harvard University Press,
     1975.

Historical study of the suffrage movement in the United
States, including biographical details of leading feminists,
descriptions of their followers, supporters and audiences.

287. Hammerton, A. J. "New Trends in the History of Working Women in
Britain." LABOR HISTORY (Australia), 31 (1976), 53-60

Examines changing attitudes toward the history of working
women and discussess recent relevant works in British
historiography.

288. Hoffman, Nancy. WOMAN'S 'TRUE' PROFESSION: VOICES FROM THE HISTORY
OF TEACHING. New York, NY: McGraw-Hill, 1981.

Documentary history of the experiences of women teachers in
attendance at the first normal schools, in the one room school
house, in the urban classroom at the turn of the century and as
teachers of freepeople in the South after the Civil War.

289. Katz, Jonathan. GAY AMERICAN HISTORY; LESBIANS AND GAY MEN IN THE
USA: A DOCUMENTARY. New York, NY: Thomas Y. Crowell, 1976.

290. Kessler-Harris, S. ALICE OUT TO WORK: A HISTORY OF WAGE-EARNING
WOMEN IN THE UNITED STATES. New York, NY: Oxford University Press,
1983.

Investigates the interconnections between women's paid and
unpaid labor and analyses the social forces that have contributed to women's lower status in the public work place.

291. Lagemann, Ellen Condliffe, ed. NURSING HISTORY: NEW PERSPECTIVES,
NEW POSSIBILITIES. New York, NY: Teacher's College Press,
Columbia University, 1983.

Collection of essays exploring the history of nursing in the
United States, its definition as an acceptable female profession and its particular situation in relation to other health
professions.

292. Lavrin, Asuncion. LATIN AMERICAN WOMEN: HISTORICAL PERSPECTIVES.
Westport, CT: Greenwood Press, 1978, 302-332.

293. Lucas, Angela. WOMEN IN THE MIDDLE AGES. New York, NY: St.
Martin's Press, 1983.

294. Norton, Mary Beth. LIBERTY'S DAUGHTER: THE REVOLUTIONARY EXPERIENCE OF AMERICAN WOMEN. Boston, MA: Little Brown, 1980.

Based on examination of the private papers and diaries of women during the revolutionary period, the author examines the role of women, exploring changes in their social and political involvement that prefigured their position in the Victorian era.

295. Pomeroy, Sarah. GODDESSES, WHORES, WIVES, AND SLAVES: WOMEN IN CLASSICAL ANTIQUITY. New York, NY: Schocken, 1975.

Reconstructs the social history of women in the Greek and Roman worlds, drawing on literature, art, archeology. Includes useful selected bibliography.

296. Rasmussen, Linda, et al. A HARVEST YET TO REAP: A HISTORY OF PRAIRIE WOMEN. Toronto: Women's Press, 1975.

297. Robertson, Priscilla. AN EXPERIENCE OF WOMEN: PATTERN AND CHANGE IN NINETEENTH-CENTURY EUROPE. Philadelphia, PA: Temple University Press, 1982.

298. Rogers, Katharine. FEMINISM IN THE EIGHTEENTH-CENTURY. Champaign, IL: University of Illinois Press, 1982.

299. Schlissel, Lillian. WOMEN'S DIARIES OF THE WESTWARD JOURNEY. New York, NY: Schocken Books, 1982.

Based on an extensive investigation of the diaries and personal correspondence of over one hundred women, the author reconstructs the experiences, attitudes and perceptions of women who went West from 1840 - 1870.

300. Schofield, Ann. "Rebel Girls and Union Maids: The Woman Question in the Journals of the AFL and IWW: 1905 - 1920." FEMINIST STUDIES, 9, 2 (Summer 1983), 335-358.

301 Smith, Hilda. SEVENTEENTH CENTURY ENGLISH FEMINISTS. Champaign, IL: University of Illinois Press, 1982.

302. Sterling, Dorothy. BLACK FOREMOTHERS: THREE LIVES. Old Westbury, NY: Feminist Press, 1979.

Explores the contributions of Ellen Craft, Ida B. Wells and Mary Church Terrell to the struggle for human rights.

303. Storm, Sharon Hartman. "Challenging the "Women's Place:" Feminism, the Lady and Industrial Unionism in the 1930s." FEMINIST STUDIES, 9, 2 (Summer 1983), 359-386.

> Investigates the union activities of women in the Depression era and addresses the question of why women's union organizing strategies have differed from men's.

304. Stuart, Susan Mosher, ed. WOMEN IN MEDIEVAL SOCIETY. Philadelphia: PA: University of Pennsylvania Press, 1976.

305. Ulrich, Laurel Thatcher. GOOD WIVES: IMAGES AND REALITIES IN THE LIVES OF WOMEN IN NEW ENGLAND: 1650-1750. New York, NY: Oxford University Press, 1983.

> Using court records, letters, diaries and gravestones, the author analyses the life of the ordinary women of the period.

306. Vicinus, Martha. A WIDENING SPHERE: CHANGING ROLES OF VICTORIAN WOMEN. Bloomington, IN: Indiana University Press, 1977.

307. Ware, Susan. BEYOND SUFFRAGE: WOMEN IN THE NEW DEAL. Cambridge, MA: Harvard University Press, 1981.

> Surveys the experiences and contributions of twenty eight women who held positions in the Roosevelt administration who entered politics through their work in social and welfare causes.

308. Welter, Barbara. DIMITY CONVICTIONS: THE AMERICAN WOMAN IN THE NINETEENTH CENTURY. Athens, OH: Ohio University Press, 1976.

> Collection of nine essays, some previously published, dealing with women and spiritualism in the works of nineteenth - century religious writers.

D. CURRICULUM STRATEGIES

309. Arron, Silvia Marina. "Teaching the History of Hispanic-American Women." HISTORY TEACHER, 13, 4 (1980), 493-507.

> Includes a discussion of issues, a course syllabus, and an annotated bibliography.

310. Bornat, Joanna. "Women's History and Oral History: An Outline and Bibliography." ORAL HISTORY, 5 (1977) 124-135.

311. Downey, Mathew. TEACHING AMERICAN HISTORY: NEW DIRECTIONS.
Washington, DC: National Council for the Social Studies, 1982.

     Chapter one reviews materials, rationale and instructional
     strategies for integrating women's history within the
     traditional course in American History.

312. Hull, Gloria T., Patricia Bell Scott, and Barbara Smith. ALL THE
WOMEN ARE WHITE, ALL THE BLACKS ARE MEN, BUT SOME OF US ARE BRAVE:
BLACK WOMEN'S STUDIES. Old Westbury, NY: Feminist Press, 1983.

     Award winning collection of essays exploring thematic issues
     for course units on Black women.

313. Lerner, Gerda. TEACHING WOMEN'S HISTORY. Washington, DC: American
Historical Association, 1980.

     Describes the rationale and objectives for the reconstruction
     of historical study. Explores new curricular materials and
     research, and proposes reform measures in course organization
     and pedagogy.

314. Moscovich, James M. "The Study of Women in Ancient Society."
HISTORY AND SOCIAL SCIENCE TEACHER, 17, 4 (Summer 1982), 211-214.

     Discusses the way in which women's roles and contributions
     can be studied in courses in ancient history. Explores the
     importance of introducing considerations of the roots of
     misogyny and the relationship between myth and sociocultural
     patterns.

315. Pierson, Ruth and Alison Prentice. "Feminism and the Writing and
Teaching of History." ATLANTIS, 7 (Spring 1982) 37-46.

316. Sanders, Beverly (Project Director). WOMEN IN AMERICAN HISTORY:
A SERIES. Washington, DC: Womens Educational Equity Act Program,
US Office of Education, 1980.

     Developed for senior high school. Projects and curriculum
     materials useful to introductory college level courses.

317. Tigges, Linda. "Women and Western Civilization: Recommendations
for Teachers." COMMUNITY COLLEGE SOCIAL SCIENCE JOURNAL, 2, 2
(1978), 6-12.

     Provides the rationale, course outline, methods and bibliography
     for the course.

VII.
FINE ARTS

The scholarship on women in the fine arts has been concentrated mainly in the field of art history. The recovery of important women artists and their work, as well as reappraisals of the way well known figures in the arts have interpreted female experience, have been major concerns. Recently, however, women in the fine arts have begun to write about their experiences as artists and teachers.

While the visual arts comprise the majority of entries in this section, resources are also cited here and in Section I, Bibliographies and Resources, for music, dance, and theatre. The first group of entries, Women in the Profession, discusses personal, social, and professional issues involved in becoming a woman artist, and in sustaining a career as a woman artist. This subsection is followed by Reconceptualizing the Discipline, which includes entries in feminist art history and art criticism. These works explain how feminist perspectives can be used to critique the values underlying artistic portrayals and interpretations of women, women's experience, and the whole of human experience. These general theories of feminist criticism are followed by the subsection, Thematic Studies, which cites works that use feminist criticism to interpret specific topics or themes. Also included here are historic studies that provide knowledge about women artists and an interpretation of their works. The last subsection, Curriculum Strategies, contains references that discuss various approaches to feminist art education.

A. WOMEN IN THE PROFESSION

318. Chiarmonte, Paula, ed. WOMEN ARTISTS: A RESOURCE AND RESEARCH GUIDE. Tuscon, AZ: Art Libraries Society of North America, 1982.

Provides information about historical and contemporary women artists found in print and non print resources and in institutional collections. Includes articles on exhibition catalogs, galleries, and performance art.

319. Greer, Germaine. THE OBSTACLE RACE: THE FORTUNES OF WOMEN PAINTERS AND THEIR WORK. New York, NY: Farrar, Strauss & Giroux, 1979.

320. Miller, Lynn F., and Sally S. Wenson. LIVES AND WORKS: TALKS TO WOMEN ARTISTS. Metuchen, NJ: Scarecrow Press, 1981.

    Interviews with 15 American women artists focusing on the development and meaning of each artist's work.

321. Placksin, Sally. AMERICAN WOMEN IN JAZZ; 1900 TO THE PRESENT: THEIR WORDS, LIVES, AND MUSIC. New York, NY: Seaview Books, 1982.

    Provides brief biographies of women jazz instrumentalists and situates their stories within the musical and social context of each decade.

322. Whitesel, Lita. "Women as Art Students, Teachers, and Artists." ART EDUCATION, 28 (March 1975), 21-26.

    Explains that pattern of education and career participation in the arts are different for males and females.

323. Zaimont, Judith Lang, Catherine Overhauser, and Jane Gottlieb. THE MUSICAL WOMAN: AN INTERNATIONAL PERSPECTIVE. Westport, CT: Greenwood Press, 1984.

    Lists women's achievements as composers, conductors, critics, scholars and entrepreneurs. Contains essays organized into eight sections dealing with aspects of the music profession and industry. Annual publication.

B. RECONCEPTUALIZING THE DISCIPLINE

324. Broude, Norma and Mary D. Garrard. FEMINISM AND ART HISTORY: QUESTIONING THE LITANY. New York, NY: Harper and Row, 1982.

325. Faxon, Alicia. "Images of Women in the Sculpture of Harriet Hosmer." WOMAN'S ART JOURNAL, 2, 1 (Spring-Summer 1981), 25-29.

326. Kampen, Natalie and Elizabeth G. Grossman. "Feminism and Methodolgy: Dynamics of Change in the History of Art and Architecture." Wellesley, MA: Wellesley College Center for Research on Women, 1983.

    Deals with the impact of feminism on methods used in the history of art and architecture.

327. Parker, Rozsika and Griselda Pollock, OLD MISTRESSES: WOMEN, ART, AND IDEOLOGY. New York, NY: Pantheon Books, 1982.

    Examines how women's art has been misrepresented and critiques the ideological basis of the writing and teaching of art history.

328. Petersen, Karen and J. J. Wilson. WOMEN ARTISTS: RECOGNITION AND REAPPRAISAL FROM THE EARLY MIDDLE AGES TO THE TWENTIETH CENTURY. New York, NY: New York University Press, 1976.

    Provides biographic sketches of western women artists by chronological periods. Includes one chapter on women artists in China.

329. Pollock, Griselda. "Women, Art and Ideology: Questions for Feminist Art Historians." WOMAN'S ART JOURNAL, 4, 1 (1983), 39-47.

330. Reinhardt, Nancy S. "New Directions for Feminist Criticism in Theatre and the Related Arts." In A FEMINIST PERSPECTIVE IN THE ACADEMY: THE DIFFERENCE IT MAKES. Elizabeth Langland and Walter Grove, eds. Chicago, IL: The University of Chicago Press, 1981, 25-51.

    Discusses a feminist approach to theatre and cinema.

331. Rom, Cristine C. "The Feminist Art Journal." WOMAN'S ART JOURNAL, 2, 2 (Fall-Winter 1981-1982), 19-24.

    Discusses the creation of THE FEMINIST ART JOURNAL in 1972, its intentions, history, and demise in 1977.

332. Rubinstein, Charlotte Streifer. AMERICAN WOMEN ARTISTS: FROM EARLY INDIAN TIMES TO THE PRESENT. Boston, MA: G. K. Hall, 1982.

    Offers a chronological overview of American women artists. Chapters begin with historical background and are followed by essays on individual artists. Includes bibliographies and appendices.

333. Russell, H. Diane. "Art History." SIGNS, 5, 3 (1980), 468-481.

    Reviews literature on women an .he visual arts. Discusses the influence of sexual politics on the study of women's imagery.

334. Sandell, Renee. "Female Aesthetics: The Women's Art Movement and Its Aesthetic Split." JOURNAL OF AESTHETIC EDUCATION, 14 (October 1980), 103-110.

    Explores opposing views of the women's art movement and the issues about which art critics differ.

335. Sherman, Claire Richter and Adele M. Holcomb, eds. "WOMEN AS INTER-PRETERS OF THE VISUAL ARTS, 1820-1979. Westport, CT: Greenwood Press, 1981.

    Supplies biographical and critical essays on careers of twelve European and American art historians, critics, educators, archaeologists, and curators. Summarizes the work of approximately 100 other women.

336. Tufts, Eleanor. "Beyond Gardner, Gombrich, and Janson: Towards a Total History of Art." ARTS MAGAZINE, LV, 8 (April 1981), 150-154.

    Argues for the inclusion of women artists such as Sofonisba, Angvisciola, Artemisia Gentileschi, Clara Peters, Rachel Ruysch, Kathe Kollwitz, Remedias Varo and Leonora Carrington in Art History books.

C. THEMATIC STUDIES

337. Brooks, George E. "Artists' Descriptions of Senegalese Signares: Insights Concerning French Racist and Sexist Attitudes in the Nineteenth Century." GENEVE-AFRIQUE, (Switzerland) 18, 1 (1980), 75-89.

    Signares, African women who headed the households of resident Frenchmen in Senegal, underwent a significant loss of status in the 19th century. A study of five artistic depictions of these women chronicles their stereotypes from the authoritative head of a large household to the sensuous and corrupting mistress of a colonial.

338. Gillespie, Patti P. "Feminist Theater." QUARTERLY JOURNAL OF SPEECH, 64, 3 (October 1978), 284-294.

    Describes the development of feminist theaters in the 1970s. Explains their characteristics and their relationship to problems addressed by the women's movement.

339. Hayden, Dolores. THE GRAND DOMESTIC REVOLUTION: A HISTORY OF FEMINIST DESIGNS FOR AMERICAN HOMES, NEIGHBORHOODS AND CITIES. Cambridge, MA: The M.I.T. Press, 1981.

Discusses the work of material feminists who sought to improve the conditions for domestic work by redesigning houses and organizing co-ops, community kitchens, and day care. Analyses the decline of material feminists in the 1930s and the relevance of their ideas for contemporary times.

340. Hoak, Dale. "Witch-Hunting and Women in the Art of the Renaissance." HISTORY TODAY (Great Britain), 31 (February 1981), 22-26.

Surveys some paintings of the Renaissance which depict witches and other minions of the Devil, usually portrayed as females.

341. Jaskoski, Helen. "'My Heart Will Go Out': Healing Songs of Native American Women." INTERNATIONAL JOURNAL OF WOMEN'S STUDIES, 4 (March-April 1981), 118-34.

Discusses the song of medicine women, women's medicine societies, and special ceremonials for women.

342. Kimball, Gayle, ed. WOMEN'S CULTURE: THE WOMEN'S RENAISSANCE OF THE SEVENTIES. Metuchen, NJ: Scarecrow Press, 1981.

Collection of twenty essays and interviews that explore women's creativity and organizations. Explores women's themes, images, and style in the visual and performing arts, and in religion, literature, and therapy.

343. Kuhn, Annette. WOMEN'S PICTURES: FEMINISM AND CINEMA. Boston, MA: Routledge and Kegan Paul, 1981.

344. Leader, Bernice Kramer. "Antifeminism in the Paintings of the Boston School." ARTS MAGAZINE, 56, 5 (1982), 112-119.

Studies the idealized figure paintings of women by the Boston School at the turn of the century. Reveals how they reflect traditional attitudes regarding women's role as domestic ornaments despite their more active role in civic and social reform.

345. Lippard, Lucy R. FROM THE CENTER: FEMINIST ESSAYS ON WOMEN'S ART. New York: Dutton, 1976.

Contains a selection of Lippard's essays and monographs on women artists and the distinctiveness of women's art. Covers sexual politics in art, household images, women's body art, female imagery, women's conceptual art, and selected feminist art institutions.

346. Seifert, Carolyn J. "Images of Domestic Madness in the Art and Poetry of American Women." WOMAN'S ART JOURNAL, 1, 2 (Fall-Winter 1980-1981), 1-6.

347. Stoddard, Karen M. SAINTS AND SHREWS: WOMEN AND AGING IN AMERICAN POPULAR FILM. Westport, CT: Greenwood Press, 1983.

>   Analyses images of older women in popular films, interprets the cultural messages conveyed through these images, and assesses their continued impact on society.

348. Tickner, Lisa. "The Body Politic: Female Sexuality and Women Artists Since 1970." ART HISTORY, 2, 2 (June 1978), 236-251.

>   Discusses recent works by women artists representing sexual aspects of the female body in relation to the tradition of western erotic art and developments in the feminist movement.

349. Wade, Jennifer. "The Chosen Few: Women Painters of the 19th Century." ART ANTIQUES, 4, 1 (1981) 26, 28, 108, 110.

>   Discusses American and European artists, including Mary Cassatt, Berthe Morisot, Cecilia Beaux, Rosa Bonheur, Lilla Cabot Perry, Martha Walter, Jane Petersen, and others.

D.   CURRICULUM STRATEGIES

350. Collins, Georgia C. "Feminist Approaches to Art Education." JOURNAL OF AESTHETIC EDUCATION, 15 (April 1981), 83-94.

>   Analyzes the problems and possibilities of three change orientations within the women's art movement and suggests that feminism is best interpreted by the art teacher as a critique of values associated with the relationship of art and women.

351. Loeb, Judy, ed. FEMINIST COLLAGE; EDUCATING WOMEN IN THE VISUAL ARTS. New York, NY: Teachers College Press, 1979.

>   Twenty-eight essays covering feminism and art, art history, women artists, art education, research in art, the status of women in art.

352. Sandell, Renee Kunowitz. "Feminist Art Education: Definition, Asessment and Application to Contemporary Art Education." Diss. Ohio State University 1978.

353. White, Barbara E. "Different Points of View about Women's Studies in Art and Art History." FEMINIST ART JOURNAL, 3 (Spring 1974), 20-21.

    Description of five different courses on women and art.

VIII.
PHILOSOPHIC AND
THEOLOGICAL PERSPECTIVES

This section contains modern works on women in philosophy and
theology. Until quite recently, with the exception of the religious
sisterhoods, women have been as underrepresented in philosophy and theology as they have been in science and technology. And, although philosophers and theologians have spoken to sex differences in their efforts
to make sense of the human condition, feminist treatises have been rare.
Recent scholarship has begun to reclaim the work of women in these fields
and reconstruct traditionally held concepts of the nature of woman in
relation to political philosophy, social and scientific ethics, moral
behavior, metaphysics, spirituality and theories of knowledge. This
important work is just beginning, however. In philosophy, feminist theory
is not yet recognized as a major movement or legitimate methodology.
Feminist philosophers tend to take an interdisciplinary perspective and
thus their works are often judged to be outside disciplinary paradigms.
Further, issues of particular significance to women - like abortion,
gender inequality, sexuality and motherhood - traditionally have not been
deemed appropriate objects for philosophic analysis.

In the subsections that follow, the situation of women in the academic disciplines of philosophy and theology, and women's professional
participation in the church, are documented in Women in the Profession.
In Reconceptualizing the Discipline works in philosophy and religion that
propose modern feminist approaches to old questions and generate new
questions are cited. Thematic Studies contains references to scholarship
dealing with particular philosophical movements and religions, as well as
works that treat issues of particular significance to women. Finally,
Curriculum Strategies includes citations for the relatively small
number of sources that present model courses of study and proposals for
pedagogy within the discipline.

A. WOMEN IN THE PROFESSION

354. Fox, Siegrun Freyss. "Political, Abstract, and Domestic Spheres:
      Why Have Women Been Underrepresented in Political Philosophy?" Diss.
      Claremont Graduate School, CA: 1978.

This thesis offers a broad explanation of why few women have become political philosophers of paradigmatic stature. Examines special constraints affecting women in this area.

355. Ruth, Sheila. "Methodocracy, Misogyny, and Bad Faith: Sexism in the Philosophical Establishment." METAPHILOSOPHY, 10 (January 1979), 48-61.

Discusses sexism in the philosophic establishment and in the very structure of its method and the logic of its criticism. Calls for feminist analysis.

356. Weidman, Judith L., ed. WOMEN MINISTERS. New York, NY: Harper and Row, 1981.

Collection of essays by clergywomen exploring changes ordained women ministers are making in seminary education, church life and the liturgy. Includes discussions of differences in women's preaching styles and approach to pastoral role and variety of problems faced by women at all stages in the profession.

357. Whitbeck, Caroline, ed. DIRECTORY OF WOMEN IN PHILOSOPHY: 1981-1982. Bowling Green, OH: Philosophical Documentation Center, 1982.

Includes two sections; one gives information on women in the profession, the other indexes women in the field by specialization.

B.   RECONCEPTUALIZING THE DISCIPLINE

358. Andolsen, Barbara Hilkert. "Agape in Feminist Ethics." JOURNAL OF RELIGIOUS ETHICS, 9 (Spring 1981), 69-83.

Feminist ethicists are now questioning the exclusive emphasis on other-regard as the content of agape and are instead posing healthy self-regard and mutuality as alternative images of love.

359. Daly, Mary. BEYOND GOD THE FATHER: TOWARD A PHILOSOPHY OF WOMAN'S LIBERATION. Boston, MA: Beacon Press, 1973.

Discusses the male bias of traditional religions and women's religious and psychological oppression. Proposes a new feminist critique and definition of spirituality.

360. _____. GYN/ECOLOGY: THE METAETHICS OF RADICAL FEMINISM. Boston, MA: Beacon Press, 1980.

Argues that men have polluted the cultural ecology of women and established gynecology as a particularly destructive symbolic ritual.

361. Eisenstein, Zillah. THE RADICAL FUTURE OF LIBERAL FEMINISM. New York, NY: Longman, 1981.

Examines the historical and philosophical significance of male bias in classical political philosophy and the origins of feminism in the works of Wollstonecraft, John Stuart Mill and Harriet Taylor.

362. English, Jane. "Philosophy." SIGNS, 3, 4 (1978), 823-831.

A bibliographical essay citing new literature on feminism, and noting feminism's greater respectability among academic philosophers.

363. Ferguson, Kathy E. SELF, SOCIETY, AND WOMANKIND: THE DIALECTIC OF LIBERATION. Westport, CT: Greenwood Press, 1980.

In this book the author creates a theory of feminism based on the views of self-other relations found in the works of George Herbert Mead and other process philosophers.

364. Fiorenza, Elizabeth Schussler. IN MEMORY OF HER: A FEMINIST THE-OLOGICAL RECONSTRUCTION OF CHRISTIAN ORIGIN. New York, NY: Cross-road Publication Company, 1983.

365. Gould Carol C. ed. BEYOND DOMINATION: NEW PERSPECTIVES ON WOMEN AND PHILOSOPHY. Totowa, NJ: Roman and Allenheld, 1983.

Collection of seventeen essays by feminist philosophers.

366. Harding, Sandra and Merrill B. Hintikka, eds. DISCOVERING REALITY: FEMINIST PERSPECTIVES ON EPISTEMOLOGY, METAPHYSICS, METHODOLOGY, AND THE PHILOSOPHY OF SCIENCE. Hingham, MA: Reidel Publishing Company, 1983.

Collection of sixteen essays by feminist philosophers addressing the topics stated in the title.

367. Jay, Nancy. "Gender and Dichotomy." FEMINIST STUDIES, 7 (Spring 1981), 38-56.

Philosophic analysis of some ways in which logical dichotomy and radical gender distinctions are linked. Argues that conceptualizing gender dictinctions in this way serves the interests of certain social groups.

368. Longino, Helen E. "Scientific Objectivity and Feminist Theorizing." LIBERAL EDUCATION, 67 (Fall 1981), 187-195.

369. Martin, Jane Roland. "Sophie and Emile: A Case Study of Sex Bias in the History of Educational Thought." HARVARD EDUCATIONAL REVIEW, 51 (August 1981).

Discusses the way philosophers have understood Rousseau's Emile as a model for educational practice without considering his provisions for female students represented in his treatment of Sophie. Argues that educational thought must include a consideration of a theorist's prescriptions for female as well as male education.

370. McMillan, Carol. WOMEN, REASON AND NATURE: SOME PHILOSOPHICAL PROBLEMS WITH FEMINISM. Princeton, NJ: Princeton University Press, 1983.

The author analyses what she takes to be the errors in feminist philosophy in contemporary approaches to nature, gender and technology and concludes that feminist theorizing as it stands will not foster human liberation.

371. Nicholson, Linda J. "'The Personal is Political': An Analysis in Retrospect." SOCIAL THEORY AND PRACTICE, 7 (Spring 1981), 85-98.

Analysis of the feminist slogan "The Personal is Political" by examining the separation of public and private spheres and the gender coding of that dichotomy.

372. Ochs, Carol. BEHIND THE SEX OF GOD: TOWARD A NEW CONSCIOUSNESS - TRANSCENDING MATRIARCHY AND PATRIARCHY. Boston, MA: Beacon Press, 1977.

Discusses the traditional split between matriarchy and patriarchy in ideals of God and spirituality. Drawing on recent psychological, sociological and anthropological works, argues for a unification of spirit and matter and an androgymous religious vision.

373. Ochshorn, Judith. THE FEMALE EXPERIENCE AND THE NATURE OF THE DIVINE. Bloomington, IN: Indiana University Press, 1981.

Examines the importance of gender in polytheism and argues that the emergence of monotheism was related to a decline in women's status in religion.

374. Pyke, Sandra and J. Martin Graham. "Gender Schema Thory and Androgyny: A Critique and Elaboration." INTERNATIONAL JOURNAL OF WOMEN'S STUDIES, 6, 1 (January 1983), 3-17.

Critiques a theoretical cognitive model of sex typing and argues that cognitive networks are related to culturally transmitted ideals of gender.

375. Robb, Carol S. "Framework for Feminist Ethics." JOURNAL OF RELIGIOUS ETHICS, 9 (Spring 1981), 48-68.

Recent foundational work in feminist ethical theory is analyzed and its contributions to the discipline of social ethics in general are discussed.

376. Sargent, Lydia. WOMEN AND REVOLUTION. Boston: MA: South End Press, 1981.

Feminist theory of the relationship between sexism and capitalism.

377. Shinell, Grace. "Towards a Feminist Metaphysics: To Hell and Back Again." WOMANSPIRIT, 6 (September 1980), 15-17.

Examines the earliest established basis of women's sacrality, reflected in votive figures and folkloric traditions associated with Bronze Age civilizations, and proposes a reappropriation of spirituality by feminists.

378. Steuernagel, Gertrude A. POLITICAL PHILOSOPHY AS THERAPY: MARCUSE RECONSIDERED. Westport, CT: Greenwood Press, 1979.

Applies the methodology of Jung to Marcuse to develop a synthesis of the two as the feminization or therapeutic reintegration of fragmented consciousness.

379. Stimpson, Catharine R. "The Mind, The Body, and Gertrude Stein." CRITICAL INQUIRY, 3, 3 (1977), 489-506.

Considers the feminization of the mind-body relationship as it found expression in Gertrude Stein's life and work.

C. THEMATIC STUDIES

380. Allen, Christine. "Sex Unity, Polarity or Complementarity?" INTER-
NATIONAL JOURNAL OF WOMEN'S STUDIES, 6, (September-October 1983),
311-325.

> Reviews philosophical treatment of sex differences and
> explores the implications of three approaches to difference.

381. Baker, Robert, and Fred Elliston, eds. PHILOSOPHY AND SEX. Buffalo,
NY: Prometheus Books, 1976.

382. Dally, Ann. INVENTING MOTHERHOOD: THE CONSEQUENCES OF AN IDEAL.
New York, NY: Schocken Books, 1983.

> The author, a British psychotherapist, investigates the history
> of child rearing and analyses the societal expectations for
> mothering and women's sense of self. Argues that feminists
> need to explore further the social and psychological implica-
> tions of motherhood.

383. Eisler, Riane, "Human Rights: An Unfinished Struggle." INTER-
NATIONAL JOURNAL OF WOMEN'S STUDIES, 6, (September-October 1983),
326-335.

> Argues that women's rights are the edge of human rights and
> that there has been an historical connection between hier-
> archical and authoritarian political systems and women's op-
> pression.

384. Elhstain, Jean Bethke. PUBLIC MAN, PRIVATE WOMAN: WOMEN IN SOCIAL
AND POLITICAL THOUGHT. Princeton, NJ: Princeton University Press,
1981.

> Analyses the treatment of women in political philosophy from
> Plato to the present and examines the implications for re-
> constructing political philosophy in light of recent feminist
> theory.

385. English, Jane, ed. SEX EQUALITY. Englewood Cliffs, NJ: Prentice
Hall, 1977.

> Collection of essays exploring the philosophical implications
> of sex equity, sex discrimination and affirmative action.

386. Falk, Nancy A. and Rita M. Gross, eds. UNSPOKEN WORLDS: WOMEN'S
RELIGIOUS LIVES IN NON-WESTERN CULTURES. New York, NY: Harper and
Row, 1980.

387. Franzosa, Susan Douglas. "Academic Freedom, Excellence and the Defense of University Autonomy." EDUCATIONAL THEORY, 31, 3-4 (Summer-Fall 1981), 359-368.

Analysis of the rhetorical claims used against affirmative action in a case involving tenure denial.

388. Gould, Carol C. and Marx W. Wartofsky. WOMEN AND PHILOSOPHY: TOWARD A THEORY OF LIBERATION. New York, NY: Putnam, 1976.

Collection of twenty-one essays by philosophers exploring feminist issues; including women's oppression, affirmative action, abortion and love. Includes an introductory essay dealing with the question of women's aptitude for philosophising.

389. Gross, Rita M., ed. BEYOND ANDROCENTRISM: NEW ESSAYS ON WOMEN AND RELIGION. Missoula, MI: Scholars Press, 1977.

390. Hoch-Smith, Judith and Anita Spring, eds. WOMEN IN RITUAL AND SYMBOLIC ROLES. New York, NY: Plenum, 1978.

391. Jagger, Alison. "Abortion and a Woman's Right to Decide." PHILOSOPHICAL FORUM, 5, 1-2 (Fall Winter 1973-1974), 347-60.

392. _____. FEMINIST POLITICS AND HUMAN NATURE. Totowa, NJ: Roman and Allenheld, 1984.

Distinguishes between liberal feminism, radical feminism, socialist feminism and Marxist feminism and investigates the implications of each.

393. Martin, Jane R. "Excluding Women from the Educational Realm." HARVARD EDUCATIONAL REVIEW, 52 (May 1982), 133-48.

Explores the significance of the neglect of women by educational philosophers and neglect of women's issues in contemporary treatments of educational thought.

394. Martin, Michael. "Preferential Hiring and the Tenuring of Teachers in the University." PHILOSOPHICAL FORUM, 5, 1-2 (Fall-Winter (1973-74), 325-33.

395. Ochs, Carol. WOMEN AND SPIRITUALITY. Totowa, NJ: Roman and Allenheld, 1983.

Philosophical investigation of theological treatments of women's spirituality.

396. O'Flaherty, Wendy. WOMEN, ANDROGYNES, AND OTHER MYSTICAL BEASTS.
      Chicago, IL: University of Chicago Press, 1980.

      The author examines the role of women in historical Hindu
      mythology.

397. Okin, Susan Mollar. WOMEN IN WESTERN POLITICAL THOUGHT. Princeton,
      NJ: Princeton University Press, 1979.

      Analyses the significance of classical political philosophers'
      assignment of women to a separate sphere and argues that
      philosophical assessments of thinkers treatments of the family
      are crucial to an understanding of their political theories.

398. Richards, Janet Radcliffe. THE SCEPTICAL FEMINIST: PHILOSOPHICAL
      INQUIRY. London: Routledge and Kegan Paul, 1980.

      Offers a philosophical analysis of contemporary feminist
      treatments of the issues of justice, equality and freedom.

399. Smith, Hilda L. REASON'S DISCIPLES: SEVENTEENTH-CENTURY FEMINISTS.
      Champaign, IL: University of Illinois Press, 1982.

400. Spretnak, Charlene, ed. THE POLITICS OF WOMEN'S SPIRITUALITY:
      ESSAYS ON THE RISE OF SPIRITUAL POWER WITHIN THE FEMINIST MOVEMENT.
      Garden City, NY: Anchor Press/Doubleday, 1982.

      Collection of essays by feminist philosophers and theologians
      exploring the conflicts between feminism and traditional
      definitions of spirituality.

401. Tong, Rosemarie. WOMEN, SEX AND THE LAW. Totowa, NJ: Roman and
      Allenheld, 1983.

      Analyses issues of relevance to women in the philosophy of the
      law.

402. Tovey, Barbara and George Tovey. "Women's PHilosophical Friends
      and Enemies." SOCIAL SCIENCE QUARTERLY, 55, 3 (1974), 586-604.

      Examines the assumptions of philosophers on the role of women,
      emphasizing Plato, Aristotle, Spinoza, Rousseau, and Mills.

403. Trebilcot, Joyce, ed. MOTHERING: ESSAYS IN FEMINIST THEORY.
      Totowa, NJ: Roman and Allenheld, 1984.

      Eighteen essays by feminist philosophers on the neglected
      topic of mothering.

404. Vetterling-Braggin, Mary. SEXIST LANGUAGE. Totowa, NJ: Little-field Adams, 1981.

> Twenty-three essays by contemporary philosophers.

405. _____ et al., eds. FEMINISM AND PHILOSOPHY. Totowa, NJ: Littlefield Adams, 1977.

> Collection of essays exploring the implications of feminist theory for the reconceptualization of traditional philosophical issues and themes.

406. _____, ed. "FEMININITY," "MASCULINITY" AND "ANDROGYNY": A MODERN PHILOSOPHICAL DISCUSSION. Totowa, NJ: Roman and Little-field, 1982.

> Collection of seventeen essays by feminist philosophers.

407. Warren, Mary Ann. THE NATURE OF WOMAN: AN ENCYCLOPEDIA AND GUIDE TO THE LITERATURE. Reyes, CA: Edgepress, 1980.

> Extensive compilation of philosophers' commentaries on women.

D. CURRICULUM STRATEGIES

408. Berman, Kathleen. "A Basic Outline for Teaching 'Women in Antiquity.'" CLASSICAL WORLD, 67, 4, (February, 1974), 213-220.

409. Christ, Carol P. and Judith Plaskow, eds. WOMAN SPIRIT RISING. New York, NY: Harper and Row, 1979.

> A collection of essays on women and religion by scholars in philosophy and theology including Mary Daly, Aviva Cantor and Merlin Stone. Thematic organization makes the anthology particularly useful for courses.

410. Gardiner, Linda. "Can This Discipline be Saved? Feminist Theory Challenges Mainstream Philosophy." Wellesley, MA: Wellesley College Center for Research on Women, 1983.

> Explores problems and suggests solutions in efforts to integrate the study of women in philosophy.

411. Garry, Ann. "Why Are Love and Sex Philosophically Interesting?" METAPHILOSOPHY, 11 (April 1980), 167-177.

412. Jagger, Allison et. al., eds. FEMINIST FRAMEWORKS. New York, NY: McGraw-Hill Book Company, 1978.

> Collection of essays by feminist scholars analysing the theoretical foundations of the liberal arts disciplines with suggestions for curriculum reform and the introduction of new thematics relevant to women.

413. Moulton, Janice. "Philosophy: Review Essay." SIGNS, 2, 2 (1976), 422-433.

> Reviews contemporary philosophical works on women and discusses the efforts of the Society for Women in Philosophy to reform the curriculum.

414. Pierce, Christine. "Philosophy: Essay Review." SIGNS 1, 2 (1975), 487-503.

> Reviews contemporary philosophical works on women and discusses sexism in philosophy texts and language.

415. Shanley, Mary L. "Invisible Women: Thoughts on Teaching Political Philosophy." NEWS FOR TEACHERS OF POLITICAL SCIENCE, 24 (1980).

> Surveys recent articles on concepts and issues in integrating women's studies into the curriculum of political philosophy courses.

416. Spann, Sylvia and M. B. Culp, eds. THEMATIC UNITS IN TEACHING ENGLISH AND THE HUMANITIES. Urbana, IL: NCTE, 1977.

> Includes a unit on women and the history of ideas.

IX.
SOCIAL SCIENCE PERSPECTIVES

The social science focus on human behavior and interaction in society has been a major source of research on the origins and maintenance
of women's oppression, a question central to feminist research. The
resources included here, with varying degrees of representation, span the
disciplines of anthropology, sociology, psychology, economics, political
science and education. As evidenced in the section on reconceptualizing
the disciplines, numerous critiques exist challenging the accuracy and
sex fairness of major methods of social science research and dominant
theories within these fields. Of special concern has been the primacy of
quantitative or positivist forms of social science research and philosophic problems associated with these methodological approaches to defining
research problems and analyzing data. Critics argue that positivist
research, with its focus on isolating variables and predicting outcomes,
fragments, trivializes, and obscures important social issues by abstract-
ing them from the context which gives them meaning. Consequently feminists assert that in addition to important contributions that quantitative research can make, qualitative, historical, and relational modes of
research and theorizing are needed within and between disciplines to
develop knowledge about women's experience and to more accurately interpret the whole of human experience.

A major theme investigated by feminists in the social sciences is
the nature and origins of sexism, the social context that perpetuates it,
and how it is related to race and class oppression. This area is an
important topic for research since knowledge of the mechanisms for main-
taining these inequities is necessary for countering their power.

Another major theme appearing in this literature is the exploration
of how women have historically worked to resist sexism and produce social
changes to improve their personal and collective situation. This research is significant because it uncovers the positive tradition of
women's social action and enlightens current efforts for social progress.

The first subsection, Women in the Profession, provides references
on the status of women within selected social science fields and historic
studies of the contributions of notable women social scientists. Reconceptualizing the Disciplines, contains entries that critique social
science research methodology and dominant theoretic frameworks, offering

alternative perspectives and paradigms on the construction of social science knowledge. The works cited in the The Social Context of Sexism, investigate the origins of women's oppression and the ideological, cultural, and psychological forces that maintain and resist sexism, classism, and racism. Women and Social Change includes research on the individual and collective roles of women in historic and contemporary efforts to promote social justice. The concluding subsection, Curriculum Strategies, contains works discussing curricular and pedagogical issues involved in integrating Women's Studies into the social sciences.

A. WOMEN IN THE PROFESSION

417. Brody, Janine. "Women in Political Science: Report on the Status of Women in the Discipline." RESOURCES FOR FEMINIST RESEARCH, 11 (November 1982), 341-348.

418. Deegan, Mary Jo. "Early Women Sociologists and the American Sociological Society: The Patterns of Exclusion and Participation." AMERICAN SOCIOLOGIST, 16 (February 1981), 14-24.

419. Evans, Judith. "Attitudes Toward Women in American Political Science." GOVERNMENT AND OPPOSITION, 15, 1 (Winter 1980), 101-114.

420. Garrison, Dee. "Karen Horney and Feminism." SIGNS, 6 (Summer 1981), 672-91.

    Discusses Horney's critique of psychoanalytic theory and the effect of cultural context on her thinking.

421. Gray, Janet Dreyfus. "The Married Professional Woman: an Examination of Her Role Conflicts and Coping Strategies." PSYCHOLOGY OF WOMEN QUARTERLY, 7 (Spring 1983), 235-243.

    Surveys 232 married women doctors, lawyers and professors regarding their attitudes toward their roles and how they cope with role conflicts.

422. O'Connell, Agnes N. and Nancy Felipe Russon, guest eds. "Eminent Women in Psychology: Models of Achievement." Special Issue. PSYCHOLOGY OF WOMEN QUARTERLY, 5 (Fall 1980).

    Special issue studying the career models and biographies of significant women in psychology.

423. Scott, Sue and Mary Potter, "On the Bottom Rung: a Discussion of Women's Work in Sociology." WOMEN'S STUDIES INTERNATIONAL FORUM, 6, 2 (1983), 211-222.

424. Shakesshaft, Carol. "Framework for Studying Schools as Work Settings for Women Leaders." Paper presented at the Annual Meeting of the American Educational Research Association, New York, NY:
March 19-23, 1982. ERIC ED 216 441.

> Presents an analysis of reasearch on women in educational
> administration and suggests a paradigm for future research on
> women in education.

B. RECONCEPTUALIZING THE DISCIPLINE

425. Acker, Sandra. "No-woman's land: British Sociology of Education."
SOCIOLOGICAL REVIEW, 29, 1 (1981), 77-104.

> The author discusses the absence of a feminist critique of the
> sociology of education and suggests what a feminist sociology
> of education might do.

426. Barrett, Nancy S. "How the Study of Women Has Restructured the
Discipline of Economics." In A FEMINIST PERSPECTIVE IN THE ACA-
DEMY: THE DIFFERENCE IT MAKES. Elizabeth Langland and Walter
Gove, eds. Chicago, IL: The University of Chicago Press, 1981,
101-109.

> Explains the impact of women's studies on the traditional
> assumptions of the mainstream or "neoclassical" school of
> economics.

427. Baumrind, Diana. "New Directions in Socialization Research."
AMERICAN PSYCHOLOGIST, 35, 7 (July 1980), 639-652.

> Concerns current challenges to the traditional, logical posi-
> tivist paradigm in socialization research by a paradigm more
> congruent with a concrete, historical, and relational mode of
> cognition.

428. Brown, Judith. "Cross-cultural Perspectives on Middle-aged Women."
CURRENT ANTHROPOLOGY, 23, 2 (1982), 143-156.

> Discusses how the study of middle-aged women has been largely
> overlooked in the cross-cultural study of human development.

429. Caufield, Mina Davis. "Universal Sex Oppression? A Critique from
Marxist Anthropology." CATALYST [Canada], 10-11 (1977), 60-77.

> Criticizes the practice in anthropology which, based on anthro-
> pological and historical data, asserts the universality of sex
> oppression. Argues for research tracing the historic con-
> nections between productive relations and the position of women.

430. Chesler, Phyllis. WOMEN AND MADNESS. Garden City, NY: Doubleday, 1972.

    Criticizes psychiatry for its failure to examine how women's unhappiness or mental illness is culturally constructed from societal patterns that encourage passivity, dependence, and self-sacrifice. Asserts that women who rebel against sex role stereotyping may be given inappropriate psychiatric treatment.

431. Chodorow, Nancy. THE REPRODUCTION OF MOTHERING: PSYCHOANALYSIS AND THE SOCIOLOGY OF GENDER. Berkeley, CA: University of California Press, 1978.

    Analyzes the question of why women in most societies assume primary responsibility for childcare. Questions prevailing biological and socio-anthropological views, and offers a feminist psychoanalytic explanation.

432. Collier, Betty and Louis Williams. "Towards a Bilateral Model of Sexism." HUMAN RELATIONS, 34, 2 (1981), 127-139.

    Questions paradigmatic assumptions that most commonly appear in anthropological literature of women's studies.

433. Dinnerstein, Dorothy. THE MERMAID AND THE MINOTAUR: SEXUAL ARRANGEMENTS AND HUMAN MALAISE. New York, NY: Harper, 1976.

    Examines the cultural pattern of exclusive female child care and its psychological consequences for sex role differences and relationships between the sexes.

434. Eichler, Margrit. "Power, Dependency, Love and the Sexual Division of Labour: A Critique of the Decision-making Approach to Family Power and an Alternative Approach with an Appendix: On Washing My Dirty Linen in Public." WOMEN'S STUDIES INTERNATIONAL QUARTERLY, 4, 2 (1981), 201-19.

    Critiques the dominant approach to theories of family power.

435. Evans, Judith. "Women and Politics: A Re-Appraisal." POLITICAL STUDIES, 28, 2 (June 1980), 210-221.

    Critically assesses traditional beliefs about women's participation in politics.

436. Field, Karen. "Alexandra Kollontai: Precursor of Eurofeminism." DIALECTICAL ANTHROPOLOGY, 6, 3 (1982), 229-244.

Identifies the exploration of the history of feminist scholarship as a major anthropological task. Studies the work of
Alexandra Kollontai, a Russian aristocrat born in 1872, for
this purpose.

437. Finkelstein, Joanne L. "Sociology and Susan Sontag: Re-shaping the
Discipline." WOMEN'S STUDIES INTERNATIONAL QUARTERLY, 4, 2 (1981),
179-90.

Questions the interpretive framework and methodological
practices of the discipline and proposes reshaping sociology
through a new perspective drawing from feminist scholarship and
the arts.

438. Firestone, Shulamith. THE DIALECTIC OF SEX: THE CASE FOR FEMINIST
REVOLUTION. New York, NY: Morrow, 1970.

Presents a radical feminist perspective on the history and
situation of women and discusses possibilities for social
transformation.

439. Fox, Siegrun Freyss. "Political, Abstract, and Domestic Spheres:
Why Have Women Been Underrepresented in Political Philosophy?"
Diss. Claremont Graduate School, CA: 1978.

See no. 354.

440. Gilligan, Carol. IN A DIFFERENT VOICE. Cambridge, MA: Harvard
University Press, 1982.

Critiques the psychology field's treatment of female psychology from Freud to Piaget. Argues that prevailing theories
of developmental psychology are inconsistent with the nature of
women's psychological experience.

441. Glennon, Lynda M. WOMEN AND DUALISM: A SOCIOLOGY OF KNOWLEDGE
ANALYSIS. New York, NY: Longman Press, 1979.

442. Kahn, Arnold and Paula Jean. "Integration and Elimination or
Separation and Redefinition: The Future of the Psychology of
Women." SIGNS, 8, 4 (1983), 659-671.

Explores different views about the advantages and dis-
advantages of mainstreaming feminist research into psychology or separating feminist research into a distinct field
on the psychology of women.

443. Miller, Jean Baker. TOWARD A NEW PSYCHOLOGY OF WOMEN. Boston, MA: Beacon Press, 1976.

    Examines the unhealthy psychological consequences of stereo-
    typical male and female characteristics. Discusses a value
    system where strength, weakness, power, emotion, and caring
    take on new meaning.

444. Millett, Kate. SEXUAL POLITICS. Garden City, NY: Doubleday, 1970.

    Analyzes the relationship between the sexes as a power struggle
    in which women are exploited. Examines how patriarchal bias
    operates through culture and how this is reflected in litera-
    ture.

445. Mitchell, Juliet. PSYCHOANALYSIS AND FEMINISM. New York, NY: Pantheon, 1974.

    Reassesses Freud's work in an effort to eliminate its sexist
    bias while retaining helpful aspects of psychoanalytic theory
    for the development of a feminist psychology of women.

446. Okin, Susan Moller. WOMEN IN WESTERN POLITICAL THOUGHT. Princeton, NJ: Princeton University Press, 1979.

447. Parlee, Mary B. "Psychology and Women." SIGNS, 5, 1 (Fall 1979), 121-133.

    Reviews the psychological literature on women and categorizes
    current work in that field into 4 types. Focuses on the
    relationship between feminist and traditional psychology.

448. Pateman, Carole, "Women and Consent." POLITICAL THEORY, 8, 2 (1980), 149-168.

    Criticizes democratic consent theorists by presenting empirical
    evidence on legal and judicial actions concerning women.

449. Roberts, Helen, ed. DOING FEMINIST RESEARCH. London: Routledge and Kegan Paul, 1981.

    A collection of papers on the possibilities and problems
    involved in conducting sociological research from a feminist
    perspective.

450. Rodnell, Sue. "Men, Women, and Sexuality: A Feminist Critique of The Sociology of Deviance." WOMEN'S STUDIES INTERNATIONAL QUARTERLY, 4, 2 (1981), 145-55.

This article critically examines a number of works by sociologists of deviance and lends support for the claim that even
radical sociology remains male-defined.

451. Rosaldo, Michelle Z. "The Use and Abuse of Anthropology: Reflections on Feminism and Cross-cultural Understanding." SIGNS, 5,
3 (1980), 389-417.

Rosaldo assesses how feminist writers incorporate anthropology
into their works and evaluates her previous work.

452. Rowbotham, Sheila, WOMAN'S CONSCIOUSNESS, MAN'S WORLD. Harmonds-
worth: Penguin, 1973.

Discusses the social and economic implications of a new
feminist consciousness and explores the historical roles of
women as producers and consumers within the capitalist state.

453. Sayers, Janet. "Biological Determinism, Psychology and the Division
of Labour by Sex." INTERNATIONAL JOURNAL OF WOMEN'S STUDIES, 3 (May-
June 1980), 241-60.

Critiques recent and nineteenth century variants of theories
bases on biologically-determined psychological differences
between the sexes.

454. Scheper-Hughes, Nancy and Mari H. Clark, guest eds. "Confronting
Problems of Bias in Feminist Anthropology." Special Issue.
WOMEN'S STUDIES, 10, 2 (1983), 109-226.

455. Shapiro, Judith. "Anthropology and the Study of Gender." In A
FEMINIST PERSPECTIVE IN THE ACADEMY: THE DIFFERENCE IT MAKES.
Elizabeth Langland and Walter Gove, eds. Chicago, IL: The Uni-
versity of Chicago Press, 1981, 110-129.

456. Stark-Adamec, Connie, J. Martin Graham, and Sandra W. Pyke.
"Androgyny and Mental Health: The Need for a Critical Evaluation of
the Theoretical Equation." INTERNATIONAL JOURNAL OF WOMEN'S STUDIES,
3 (September-October, 1980), 490-507.

Agrees with the need for an alternative to traditional sex-role
stereotyping but critiques current theories of androgyny and
argues that there are not viable alternatives.

457. Steuernagel, Gertrude A. POLITICAL PHILOSOPHY AND THERAPY: MARCUSE
RECONSIDERED. Westport, CT: Greenwood Press, 1979.

See no. 378.

458. Stock, Wendy, et al. "Women and Psychotherapy." INTERNATIONAL
     JOURNAL OF MENTAL HEALTH, 11, 1-2 (1982), 135-158.

     Considers the patriarchal structure of psychiatric institutions
     and psychological theories. Discusses the function, per-
     spective, and methods of feminist therapy. Includes biblio-
     graphy.

459. Targ, Dena B. "Ideology and Utopia in Family Studies Since the
     Second World War." WOMEN'S STUDIES INTERNATIONAL QUARTERLY, 4,
     2 (1981), 191-200.

     Critiques the conceptual frameworks of ideology and utopia in
     family studies.

460. Tiffany, Sharon W. "Women, Power, and the Anthropology of Politics:
     a Review." INTERNATIONAL JOURNAL OF WOMEN'S STUDIES, 2 (September-
     October 1979).

     This article questions the prevailing view of women and
     politics by examining the nature of power and authority and
     cross-cultural variation in female political participation.

461. Walker, Stephen and Len Barton, eds. GENDER, CLASS AND EDUCATION.
     Sussex, England: The Falmer Press, 1983.

     Develops sociological theories of education that include gender
     and class analysis. Uses the theories to study issues regard-
     ing teaching, curriculum and policy.

462. Westkott, Marcia. "Feminist Criticism of the Social Sciences."
     HARVARD EDUCATIONAL REVIEW, 49, 4 (1979), 422-430.

     Presents a feminist critique of the methods used in the social
     sciences to interpret women's experiences. Discusses alterna-
     tive approaches to research and to the selection and organiza-
     tion of content in the social sciences.

463. Young, Iris. "Socialist Feminism and the Limits of Dual Systems
     Theory." SOCIALIST REVIEW, 10, 2-3 (March-June 1980), 169-188.

     Questions the dual system theory of women's oppression based
     on the male domination of the mode of production.

C. SPECIAL ISSUES

THE SOCIAL CONTEXT OF SEXISM

464. Acker, Sandra, ed. WORLD YEARBOOK OF EDUCATION 1984: WOMEN AND
EDUCATION. New York, NY: Nichols Publishing, 1984.

> Examines the social, political, and economic context of
> education and how it affects the lives and roles of women.
> Discusses how women can use education to improve their lives.

465. Anderson, Margaret L. THINKING ABOUT WOMEN: SOCIALIST AND FEMINIST
PERSPECTIVES. New York, NY: Macmillan, 1983.

466. Davis, Angela Yvonne. WOMEN, RACE AND CLASS. New York, NY:
Random House, 1981.

> Shows the relationship of black liberation and the women's
> rights movements from slavery to the present. Discusses
> white middle class bias in the women's rights movements,
> Communist women, the "myth of the black rapist," and
> contemporary women's issues in light of historical data.

467. Eisenstein, Zillah, ed. CAPITALIST PATRIARCHY AND THE CASE FOR
SOCIALIST FEMINISM. New York, NY: Monthly Review Press, 1979.

> Discusses the relationship between sexism and capitalism
> and attempts to formulate a theory of socialist feminism.
> Provides accounts of socialist feminist historical analysis,
> studies of women and work, and examples of socialist feminism
> in revolutionary societies and in America.

468. Hooks, Bell. AIN'T I A WOMAN: BLACK WOMEN AND FEMINISM. Boston,
MA: South End Press, 1981.

> Explores the impact of racism and sexism on black women in
> the nineteenth and twentieth centuries.

469. Kuhn, Annette and Ann Marie Wolpe, eds. FEMINISM AND MATERIALISM:
WOMEN AND MODES OF PRODUCTION. New York, NY: Routledge and Kegan
Paul, 1980.

> Collection of essays by British social scientists exploring
> the social conditions of women's work in the family and paid
> labor force in Europe and The Third World.

470. Mahdavi, Shireen. "Women and the Shii Ulama in Iran." MIDDLE
EASTERN STUDIES, 19, 1 (1983), 17-37.

Traces the variations in the degree of inequality women have experienced in Iran from ancient time to the present day. Explores the role of religion as an aspect of the social context of sexism.

471. Mead, Margaret. "Women in the International World." JOURNAL OF INTERNATIONAL AFFAIRS, 30, 2 (1976-77).

472. Nash, June C., and Helen Icken Safa, eds. SEX AND CLASS IN LATIN AMERICA. New York, NY: Praeger, 1976.

473. Neal, Marie Augusta: "Women in Religious Symbolism and Organization." SOCIAL INQUIRY, 49, 2-3 (1979), 218-250.

Focuses on how Christianity has used women as religious symbols and on how women's roles have been interpreted because of religious symbolism. Discusses the effect of women's emancipation on their status in religious organizations.

474. OFF OUR BACKS. Special issue on racism and sexism. 9, 10 (November 1979).

Articles exploring the links between racism and sexism, and discrimination against homosexuals.

475. Sargent, Lydia. WOMEN AND REVOLUTION. Boston, MA: South End Press, 1981.

See no. 376.

476. Sokoloff, Natalie. BETWEEN MONEY AND LOVE: THE DIALECTICS OF WOMEN'S HOME AND MARKET WORK. New York, NY: Praeger, 1980.

Discusses women's oppression in the home and in the labor force as a consequence of patriarchy in Western capitalist economic systems.

477. Tax, Meredith. THE RISING OF THE WOMEN: FEMINIST SOLIDARITY AND CLASS CONFLICT, 1880-1917. New York, NY: Monthly Review Press, 1981.

Discusses the different relationship of the women's movement to middle class and working class women and studies the history of interaction between the labor movement and the women's rights movement around the turn of the century.

478. Torrey, Jane W. "Racism and Feminism: Is Women's Liberation for Whites Only?" PSYCHOLOGY OF WOMEN QUARTERLY, 4 (Winter 1979), 281-93.

Explores the relationships of racism, classism, and sexism.

479. Zak, Michele Wander and Patricia A. Moots, eds. WOMEN AND THE POLITICS OF CULTURE. New York, NY: Longman Press, 1983.

Provides selections of philosophic, political, and psychological literature on women from over 140 writers. Introductory essays examine the political, social, and economic contexts that have influenced feminist thought at various historical periods.

WOMEN AND SOCIAL CHANGE

480. Black, Naomi and Ann Baker Cottrell, eds. WOMEN AND WORLD CHANGE: EQUITY ISSUES IN DEVELOPMENT. Beverly Hills, CA: Sage Publications, 1981.

Discusses social policy on sex roles from a cross national perspective and analyses the contributions that social science can make to policy affecting the progress of women.

481. Cassell, Joan. A GROUP CALLED WOMEN: SISTERHOOD AND SYMBOLISM IN THE FEMINIST MOVEMENT. New York, NY: David McKay, 1977.

Analyzes group formation and organization among women. The study investigates the process of becoming a feminist and examines the structure of the women's movement in the early 70's.

482. Chodorow, Nancy and Sue Contratto. "The Fantasy of the Perfect Mother." In RETHINKING THE FAMILY: SOME FEMINIST VIEWS. Barie Thorne, ed. New York, NY: Longman Press, 1981.

483. Dill, Bonnie Thornton. "Race, Class, and Gender: Prospects for All-inclusive Sisterhood." FEMINIST STUDIES, 9, 1 (1983), 131-150.

Examines the concept of sisterhood across racial and class differences to suggest political strategies for the development of a more inclusive women's movement.

484. Donaldson, Mike. "Marx, Women and the Bourgeois Right: Feminism and Class Reconsidered." AUSTRALIA AND NEW ZEALAND JOURNAL OF SOCIOLOGY, 14, 2 (June 1978), 131-138.

Attempts to identify the class nature of the contemporary feminist struggle.

485. Finkler, K. "Dissident Religious Movements in the Service of Women's Power." SEX ROLES, 7 (May 1981), 481-96.

486. Hafkin, Nancy H., and Edna G. Bay, eds. WOMEN IN AFRICA: STUDIES IN SOCIAL AND ECONOMIC CHANGE. Stanford, CA: Stanford University Press, 1976.

487. Hahner, June. "Feminism, Women's Rights, and the Suffrage Movement in Brazil." LATIN AMERICAN RESEARCH REVIEW. 15, 1 (1980), 65-111.

Reviews the suffrage movement in Brazil. Examines nineteenth century social conditions, women's education, the Brazilian feminist press, women's associations, and the abolition movement.

488. Harding, Susan. "Family Reform Movements: Recent Feminism and Its Opposition." FEMINIST STUDIES, 7 (Spring 1981), 57-75.

Discusses the ideological conflict among American women over feminist ideas and reforms.

489. Howe, Florence. WOMEN AND THE POWER TO CHANGE. New York, NY: McGraw Hill, 1975.

See no. 63.

490. Jennings, M. Kent, and Barbara G. Farah. "Ideology, Gender and Political Action: A Cross-National Survey." BRITISH JOURNAL OF POLITICAL SCIENCE, 10, 2 (April 1980), 219-240.

This paper compares men and women according to levels of ideological thinking and the conversion of this resource into varied forms of political action.

491. Kelly, Gail P. and Carolyn M. Elliot, eds. WOMEN'S EDUCATION IN THE THIRD WORLD: COMPARATIVE PERSPECTIVES. Albany, NY: State University of New York Press, 1982.

Discusses the social control function of education systems with regard to the education of women and also explores their potential to improve women's lives.

492. Lemkau, Jeanne Parr. "Personality and Background Characteristics of Women in Male-dominated Occupations: A Review." PSYCHOLOGY OF WOMEN QUARTERLY, 5 (Winter 1979), 221-40.

493. Rosaldo, Michelle and Louise Lamphere, eds. WOMEN, CULTURE AND SOCIETY. Stanford, CA: Stanford University Press, 1974.

    Presents one psychological and sixteen anthropological essays on the nature of sex roles in different societies.

494. Schofield, Ann. "Rebel Girls and Union Maids; The Woman Question in the Journals of the AFL and IWW, 1905-1920." FEMINIST STUDIES, 9, 2 (1983), 335-358.

    Contrasts the ideological implications of the AFL and IWW approaches to women's issues from 1905 to 1920. Documents how trade unions have historically perpetuated conventional attitudes concerning women's role in the home and in the workplace.

495. Smedley, Agnes. PORTRAITS OF CHINESE WOMEN IN REVOLUTION. Old Westbury, NY: Feminist Press, 1976.

496. Strom, Sharon Hartman. "Challenging 'Woman's Place': Feminism, the Left, and Industrial Unionism in the 1930s." FEMINIST STUDIES, 9, 2 (1983), 359-386.

    Examines the economic, ideological, and political variables that impeded women's efforts at labor union organization.

497. "The Tie That Binds." Special Issue. WOMEN: A JOURNAL OF LIBERATION, 6, 3 (1979).

    Explores the double binds women experience in relationships and work.

498. William, Juanita H. "Equality and the Family." INTERNATIONAL JOURNAL OF WOMEN'S STUDIES, 3 (March-April 1980), 131-42.

    Investigates social changes that occur in families that value egalitarian relationships.

D.   CURRICULUM STRATEGIES

499. BLACK STUDIES/WOMEN'S STUDIES: AN OVERDUE PARTNERSHIP. Amherst, MA: The Black Studies/Women's Studies Faculty Development Project, 1983.

Compliles course syllabi in the social sciences and humanities addressing issues of race, gender, and culture.

500. Burke, Judith Lee. "Suggestions for a Sex-fair Curriculum in Family Treatment." JOURNAL OF EDUCATION FOR SOCIAL WORK, 18, 2 (1982), 98-102.

Provides suggestions for achieving equity for women in family treatment education.

501. Curtis, Rebecca C., et al. "Sex, Fear of Success, and the Perceptions and Performance of Law School Students." AMERICAN EDUCATIONAL RESEARCH JOURNAL, 12 (SUMMER 1975), 287-97.

Discusses achievement related to attitudes and behaviors of male and female students. Findings indicate that women may be more likely than men to fear rejection, but not to fear success.

502. Deatherage-Newsome, Marie. "Teaching Woman's Role in Changing the Face of the Earth: How and Why." JOURNAL OF GEOGRAPHY, 77, (September-October 1978), 166-72.

Describes the content development, and structure of a one-year college geography course focusing on women's role in geography.

503. Diangson, Pat, Diane F. Kravetz and Judy Lipton. "Sex Role Stereotyping and Social Work Education." JOURNAL OF EDUCATION FOR SOCIAL WORK, 11 (August 1975), 44-49.

Examines the effect of social work education on sex distribution in types of social work practice. Discusses policy and curriculum changes to eliminate sexism.

504. Dorenkamp, Angela G. "Resisting Closure: Integrating the Humanities and Social Sciences." Paper presented at the Annual Meeting of the College English Association, Houston, TX: April 15-17, 1982. ERIC ED 217 492.

Develops an interdisciplinary approach to a women's studies course, "Images," using a paradigm informed by the fundamental differences between the aims and outlooks of the humanities and social sciences.

505. Drake, Christine. "Teaching about Third World Women." JOURNAL OF GEOGRAPHY, 82, 4 (1983), 163-169.

Studies the inequitable position, problems, and potential of
third world women. Provides a rationale, outline, and
resource list for such a course.

506. Freedman, Rita J., et al. "Mainstreaming the Psychology of Women
into the Core Curriculum." TEACHING OF PSYCHOLOGY, 9, 3 (1982)
165-168.

Discusses how some issues taught in psychology of women
courses can be included in statistics and social, developmental, and introductory psychology courses.

507. Gappa, Judith M. and Janice Pearce. SEX AND GENDER IN THE SOCIAL
SCIENCE: REASSESSING THE INTRODUCTORY COURSE. Washington, DC:
American Sociological Association, 1981.

508. Iglitzin, Lynne B. "Teaching Political Science: A Feminist Perspective." TEACHING POLITICAL SCIENCE, 5, 4 (July 1978), 385-403.

Delineates a feminist perspective within political science and
its influence on political science teaching.

509. Johnson, Marilyn, ed. "Teaching Psychology of Women." Special
Issue. PSYCHOLOGY OF WOMEN QUARTERLY, 7, 1 (1982).

510. Kravetz, Diane. "An Overview of Women for the Social Work Curriculum." JOURNAL OF EDUCATION FOR SOCIAL WORK, 18, 2, (1982), 42-
49.

511. Rosenthal, Naomi. "The Psychology of Women." PSYCHOHISTORY REVIEW,
8, 4 (1980), 32-36.

Summarizes textbooks dealing with the psychology of women
written during the past decade and describes three theoretical
perspectives that dominate them.

512. Russo, N. F., and N. J. Malovich. ASSESSING THE INTRODUCTORY PSYCHO-
LOGY COURSE. Washington, DC: American Psychological Association,
1982.

513. Terry, James L. "Bringing Women. . . In: A Modest Proposal."
TEACHING SOCIOLOGY, 10 (January 1983), 251-261.

Discusses the absence of women sociological theorists in the
history of sociology and explains how the contributions of
Harriet Martineau and Charlotte Gilman can be integrated into
a sociology course.

514. Vedovato, Sandra L. And Reesa M. Vaughter. "Psychology of Women Courses Changing Sexist and Sex-typed Attitudes." PSYCHOLOGY OF WOMEN QUARTERLY, 4 (Summer 1980), 587-90.

      Investigates the changes in sexist attitudes while partici-pating in psychology of women courses.

DIRECTORY OF SOURCES

American Anthropological Association
Committee of the Status of Women
1703 New Hampshire Avenue, N.W.
Washington, DC 20009

American Association for the
Advancement of Science
Office of Opportunity in Science
1776 Massachusetts Avenue, N.W.
Washington, DC 20036

American Educational
Research Association
1126 16th Street, N.W.
Washington, DC 20036

American Historical Association
Committee on Women Historians
400 A Street, S.E.
Washington, DC 20003

American Jewish Committee
Institute on Pluralism and
Group Identity
165 E. 56th Street
New York, NY 10022

American Psychological Association
Office of Women's Programs
1200 17th Street, N.W.
Washington, DC 20036

American Sociological Association
Teaching Resources Center
1722 N. Street, N.W.
Washington, DC 20036

Association of American Colleges
Project on the Status and
Education of Women
1818 R. Street, S.W.
Washington, DC 20009

Commission on the Status of Women
University of New Hampshire
Durham, NH 03824

Educational Development Center
EDC/Women's Educational Equity Act
55 Chapel Street
Newton, MA 02160

Great Lakes Women's Studies
Association
5500 North St. Louis Avenue
Northeastern Illinois University
Chicago, IL 60625

Lawrence Hall of Science
Occasional Papers on Women
in Science
University of California
Berkeley, CA 94720

Measurement Service Center
University of Minnesota
Minneapolis, MN 56267

Modern Language Association
of America
Commission on the Status of
Women in the Profession
62 Fifth Avenue
New York, New York 10011

National Association of Women's
Deans, Administrators and Counselors
1028 Connecticut Avenue, N.W.
Washington, DC 20036

National Council for the
Social Studies
Special Interest Group
for History Teachers
3615 Wisconsin Avenue, N.W.
Washington, DC 20016

National Council of Teachers
of Mathematics
1906 Association Drive
Reston, VA 22091

National Institute of Education
Papers on Education and Work
1211 Connecticut Avenue, N.W.
Suite 301
Washington, DC 20036

National Science Teacher's Association
1742 Connecticut Avenue, N.W.
Washington, DC 20009

New York Academy of Science
2 East 63rd Street
New York, NY 10021

Occasional Papers in Women's Studies
358 Lorch Hall
University of Michigan
Ann Arbor, MI 48109

Philosophical Documentation Center
Women in Philosophy
Bowling Green State University
Bowling Green, OH 43403

Southwest Institute for Research
on Women
University of Arizona
Tucson, AR 85306

Wellesley College Center for
Research on Women
828 Washington Avenue
Wellesley, MA 02182

Women's Studies
Resources on Women and Research
Storrs, CT 06268

Women's Studies and a Balanced
Curriculum Conference Reports
Claremont Colleges
Claremont Graduate School
169 Harper Hall
Claremont, CA 91711

AUTHOR INDEX

Co-authors as well as first authors are listed below. References are to item numbers rather than pages.

About the Compilers

SUSAN DOUGLAS FRANZOSA is an Assistant Professor of the Philosophy of Education at the University of New Hampshire. She has contributed to *Educational Theory* and *Contemporary Education.*

KAREN A. MAZZA is an Assistant Professor of Education at the University of New Hampshire. Her articles have appeared in *Journal of Curriculum Theorizing.*